Killer Doctor : The True Story of Wendi Mae Davidson

Ruthie Carter

Published by Trellis Publishing, 2021.

While every precaution has been taken in the preparation of this book, the publisher assumes no responsibility for errors or omissions, or for damages resulting from the use of the information contained herein.

KILLER DOCTOR : THE TRUE STORY OF WENDI MAE DAVIDSON

First edition. June 30, 2021.

ISBN: 979-8224139767

Written by Ruthie Carter.

A KILLER DOCTOR

THE TRUE STORY OF WENDI MAE DAVIDSON
RUTHIE CARTER

7777 **Ranch's Stock Tank**

Sometime past 11 p.m. on March 5, 2005, ranch owner Terrell Sheen received a call from Texas Ranger Shawn Palmer. Palmer explained that new information had surfaced regarding Michael Severance's disappearance, and that they needed his permission to search his property, 7777 Ranch. Sheen accepted the request, and they agreed to meet at the site, which had since been secured by police officers.

At 5.30 a.m. on March 6th, Palmer arrived at the ranch, parked by a barn and waited for the arrival of other officers. He was soon joined by Detective Dennis McGuire, and the two stood by the stock tank, with Palmer videotaping the scene. At 9 a.m., San Angelo Police Department evidence technician Rosalind Hinds and ranch owner Terrell Sheen showed up. United States Air Force Office of Special Investigations Special Agents Greg McCormick and Arch Harner arrived at the scene fifteen minutes later with their evidence technician, Julie Lecea. Sheen signed the consent-to-search form and Hinds videotaped the area, including the ranch entrance, one-way road, and the pond.

At around 10 a.m., Sergeant David Jones of the Texas Department of Public Safety, Tom Green County Sheriff's Office investigators, San Angelo Police Department and the state trooper dive team arrived at the scene. Half an hour later, the underwater crew was ready to dive into the stock tank to search for Michael Severance. At around 2 p.m., the divers discovered a body submerged in the middle of the pond, near a wire fence that cut through the middle. The body was weighed down by various objects, and attempts to film the underwater operation failed.

Once the divers detached the cinder block, tire rim, brake drum and boat anchor attached to the body, it floated up to the surface. Palmer, McGuire and Hinds, who had made their way to the middle of the pond in a boat with a team of divers, helped guide the body back to shore. The body was that of a white male in maroon boxers, and Palmer quickly identified the body as that of Michael Severance. The search was finally over.

Michael Severance

Leslie Severance joined the United States Air Force in 1976 and worked as a jet engine mechanic at Loring Air Force Base in Maine. While on leave at around Christmas time in 1976, he went to visit his aunt in Danforth, Maine, where his cousin introduced him to Valerie Smith, a New Jersey native who'd lived in Maine for only five years. The two got married in 1978. In 1980, when Valerie was pregnant with their first child, Leslie decided to leave the Air Force and they moved to Winn, a town with a population of only 400. Michael Severance was born on July 20 1980. Their second son, Frank, was born in December 1982.

Michael soon earned the name Bicycle Mike. He was always on his bike, and according to Leslie, fascinated by speed from a very young age. At 6 years, he competed in the bike race on Children's Day at the 136th annual Springfield Fair and came in third place. In 1987, the family moved near Lee, a town with a population of 800. In late February 1995, Valerie passed away. Michael was only 14.

In July of 1996, Leslie and Brinda Leighton moved in together, and Mike suddenly found himself with two new sisters, 10-year-old Brooke and 13-year-old Nicole. While Frank was a bit withdrawn, the four children got along fine. During this time, Michael was attending Lee Academy and was excelling as an athlete. Instead of choosing one skiing event to participate in, Michael partook in all three; slalom, downhill, and cross country. He excelled in all three. Despite his athletic nature, Michael Severance was an introvert, yet his quiet nature had a funny side to it, and was known to pull stunts from time to time. On prom night, he drove a big rig onto the headmaster's lawn, the highlight of the night for other students. One time he skipped class and went fishing. Later, he reported himself to the headmaster, and even gave him the fish he had caught.

After high school, Michael expressed his interest in driving semis, got his class-one license, and was hoping to get a job running short-haul routes. Leslie had no objection, but suggested that he join the armed forces. On September 28 1998, Michael started active duty in the Air Force, and was stationed at the Dyess Air Force Base in Abilene, Texas. In the aftermath of 9-11, Michael was deployed to Uzbekistan at Karshi-Khanabd Air Base. As a C-130 crew chief, his role was to ferry people and supplies into Afghanistan. Michael was always first to volunteer for the runs, and at one point his commander asked him to let others also go for the dangerous missions. In total, Michael was deployed to the Middle East five times.

In his spare time, Michael took up two-step dancing as well as racing all-terrain vehicles. In the summer of 2003, he decided to try his hand at West Texas dirt track racing and traded in his Raptor 4-wheel all-terrain vehicle for a race car he was going to use in the Modified Stock Racing. His love for speed saw him saving up for repairs, and sometimes even living on ramen noodles just to save up for spare parts. Shortly before Thanksgiving in 2003, Michael Severance went to a bar with friends for a few beers. He did not return home that night, and instead spent the night in Wendi Mae Davidson's bed.

Wendi Mae Davidson

Judy Elliott was born on November 23 1953, and grew up in Mertzon, a town with a population of 800. Lloyd Davidson had been born a few months earlier, on March 14 1953. The two met and married in 1974. Judy and Lloyd had both never been outside West Texas, and country life was all they knew. On July 23 1978, the couple welcomed their first child, Wendi Mae. The next year, on September 10, Marshall Anthony was born.

The Davidson family was a close knit one, and they were fiercely dedicated to each other. When Judy was diagnosed with lupus, she quit her job and focused on the children. She was on Social Security Disability and was therefore able to chip in financially from time to time. In their compound, Lloyd built an aviary, and stocked it with pigeons, parakeets, and cockatiels. Their household was home to a number of animals, and by age 7 Wendi had decided that she wanted to become a veterinarian.

Wendi excelled in her agricultural studies and animal science classes when she was in high school. She was a cheerleader, and also played basketball and volleyball. However, Wendi had poor social skills, and was unaware of the impact her actions and words had on the people around her. She was unable to relate well with other students, and was not a popular girl in school. To raise funds for college, she showed goats at the Tom Green County, San Angelo and Odessa Stock Shows. Despite her best efforts, she graduated salutatorian, a fete that did not make her happy.

In the fall of 1996, Wendi started college at Angelo State University and during summer breaks, worked at the North Concho Veterinary Clinic. At the time, Marshall, who was still in high school, spent his summers doing maintenance work for Dr. Terrell Sheen, a veterinarian at the time. In 1998, Lloyd found out that the Levi Strauss' plant that he had been working at for over 20 years was about to be shut down. Marshall, in a bid to help his dad, introduced him to Terrell Sheen, who hired Lloyd to be his contractor. Lloyd subsequently became a self-employed contractor, and the bulk of the work he did was for Dr. Sheen.

After high school, Marshall joined the Angelo State University, but did not find Wendi there. In a record two years' time, Wendi had completed all her prerequisite courses and had been admitted at Texas A&M, the only College of Veterinary Medicine in the state. Wendi plunged into her studies, and was a little bit social. She first became pregnant in her fourth year in campus, a pregnancy she terminated. She became pregnant a second time, and this time she carried it to full term. Tristan was born on October 29, 2001. When asked about the father of her first child, Wendi has never provided a name to date. The candidates had been Ryan Reitz and Jason Burdine, but Wendi had informed both men that the DNA test excluded both of them. She graduated from college on May 10, 2002.

After graduation, Wendi got a job as a veterinarian at Abilene Animal Hospital, a clinic that was later purchased by Dr. Larry Ellis. Dr. Ellis quickly found Wendi to be a difficult employee as she would always throw tantrums whenever animals were scheduled to be euthanized, and would always ignore Dr. Ellis' directives about how to perform various procedures. Despite Ellis' thirty year experience, Wendi always seemed to think that she knew best. Sometime in this period, Wendi found out that she was pregnant again. She terminated it.

Wendi went out one night before Thanksgiving. At the bar, the 25-year-old met 23-year-old Michael Severance, and the two went back to her place.

Wendi's professional life was less than ideal. After defying her employer's wishes on more than one occasion, she finally went too far. She failed to euthanize a litter of kittens that had feline ringworms. She took them home, putting Tristan's life in danger considering how contagious the fungal infection was. She brought the kittens back to the clinic, and as a result, twenty eight cats had to be euthanized since they had also contracted the infection. Dr. Ellis had no option but to fire her. Wendi moved to Lubbock, where she got a job with Dr. Gary Schwede. Shortly after the move, she discovered that she was pregnant.

Wendi & Michael

Wendi called Michael and informed him that he was going to be a father. At 23, he had not yet considered settling down, but wanted to do the right thing. He called his father, Leslie, who assured him that he would support any decision Michael made. Michael decided that he was going to marry Wendi. He talked it over with her, and they decided that they would wait until the baby was born.

In April 2004, Wendi took Michael to meet her parents. Judy immediately took an instant dislike to Michael. When Wendi broke the news of her pregnancy to her parents, the reception was less than enthusiastic, and even the news that he was going to marry Wendi did nothing to placate Judy's hostility towards Michael. She made her animosity towards Michael clear, and kept telling Wendi that he was "rude, disrespectful, and lazy." It was obvious that she did not find Michael a good fit for her daughter.

The relationship was far from ideal. Michael rarely went to Lubbock to visit Wendi, and she started suspecting that he was backing out of their arrangement. She called her brother Marshall and complained at length. Marshall, on his part, reminded Wendi that their mom didn't like Michael and that the marriage was not something that had to happen. It was apparent that Judy had been telling everyone in their family how much she despised Michael.

Wendi's professional life was almost in shambles again. She knew she was about to get fired, and started making plans to move back to San Angelo near her parents. This time, she would open her own clinic near Grape Creek, where her parents lived. She enlisted the help of her parents, her brother and retired veterinarian Terrell Sheen. Sheen purchased retired Dr. Freddy Miller's clinic building in Sherwood Way and rented it out to Wendi at a low cost of $1,500 per month, Lloyd and Judy invested $40,000 for renovations, and Marshall purchased supplies.

While the clinic had live-in quarters, Wendi and Michael could not live there while the renovations were being carried out. They decided to move in with Lloyd and Judy. This was a bad idea. While Michael had to commute ninety miles each day to work at the Dyess Air Force Base in Abilene, nobody seemed to appreciate this immense sacrifice. Judy's resentment of Michael grew, and Lloyd and Judy did not respect the couple's privacy. One day, Michael had switched off Tristan's baby monitor so that he and Wendi could enjoy some time alone in the bedroom. When they came out, he discovered that someone had switched it back on.

Wendi's second son, Shane, was born on September 1 2004, and in response, Judy stated, "I'd like to send that little bastard to where he came from." Soon after, Wendi, Michael, Tristan, and Shane moved into the one bedroom apartment inside the clinic building. The two set the wedding for September 13 2004. Leslie Severance came to visit his son before the wedding and to his disappointment, was treated poorly by his son's future in-laws. Lloyd would not shake his hand, and Judy wouldn't even look in his direction. He couldn't help but wonder what his son had gotten himself into.

The wedding was held at the Precinct 4 Justice of Peace office, with Judge Eddie Howard presiding. In attendance were 3-year-old Tristan, 12-day-old Shane, Leslie, Judy, and Lloyd. Deputy Linda Moore was also in attendance as the official witness. After the wedding, the attendees were to meet at Zentner's Daughter Steak House on Knickerbocker Road. However, Judy and Lloyd, who had left with Tristan after the ceremony, failed to show up. Wendi did not share the reason her parents had given her. Once in Maine, Leslie shared with his family that he did not understand how his son put up with such treatment.

January 15, 2005

On Thursday January 13, Michael was helping Wendi at the clinic when they got into a heated argument. In response, Michael took the two boys and they went to Abilene to visit his friends at the race track. He was home by 4.30 p.m., and Judy quickly took the boys to her home. Michael did not appreciate the fact that Judy was keeping the children overnight more nights of the week than they were.

Michael, Wendi, and the two boys were planning to travel to Maine to visit Leslie and the family. To celebrate their last night before the trip, Wendi and Michael decided to go out on Friday night. Once again, Judy took the children, even though she had had them the previous night and Wendi had offered to leave the kids with Jamie Crouch, Wendi's part-time employee at the clinic. The couple first stopped to have dinner at Buffalo Wild Wings, and left the restaurant at 7.40 p.m. They later went to Graham Central Station, a bar located across the street from the clinic. They had some drinks, and spent their night dancing. Later, they went back home. Michael was in good spirits, and was excited about the upcoming trip to Maine. He even drove his truck in circles in the parking lot. The events of the next 24 hours are still unclear, but this is what the state of Texas was able to reconstruct from its investigation.

When she went into the house, Wendi poured Michael a beer. She then dropped five veterinary phenobarbital pills into his drink. The strong taste of the beer was able to mask the medicinal taste of the pills, and Michael cheerfully drank his beer. The dose Wendi administered was far from fatal. However, it was enough to incapacitate Michael for up to 12 hours. Michael then undressed and collapsed on the bed. Once Wendi was sure he was unconscious, she slammed a syringe full of Beuthanasia-D into his heart. Beuthanasia-D is a veterinary euthanizing solution containing a lethal dose of pentobarbital diluted with phenytoin. Now all she had to do was wait until the drugs shut down his heart and respiratory function.

Once she confirmed he was dead, she put into action her disposal plan. Using Michael's truck, she loaded him into the truck's bed, a fete that was made easy because the uneven terrain of the parking lot made the gate panel only a mere 2 feet high. She dragged his body into the truck's bed and then went looking for items to weigh the body down. She got an old brake drum, a concrete block, as well as a spool of baling wire and a reel of fishing line. She got into the cab of the truck and made her way to Terrell Sheen's 7777 Ranch. The Davidson's relationship with Sheen saw to it that they all had keys to the ranch's gate. Wendi entered the property and drove up to the stock tank. In Texas, a stock tank refers to a large pond.

She parked the truck and got out. She dragged Michael's body onto the wooden platform which was built over the edge of the tank. She then took the balling wire and looped it around his neck. On the other end, she attached the brake drum. She then took the fishing wire, attached it to the concrete block, and then fastened it onto Michael's left leg. She rolled the body into the water, got in the truck and drove back home. At 8 a.m. Saturday morning, Wendi opened up her clinic as usual, and told her mother that Michael was too hangovered that day to help them. Sometime later, Wendi canceled the $1,500 airline tickets to Maine.

On Sunday at 5 a.m., Wendi called the Severance residence and spoke to Brinda, asking her if she'd seen or spoken to Michael. She claimed that she was still packing and Michael hadn't shown up at home since Saturday. Brinda the called the airline and found out that the tickets had been canceled. She checked in with the bus lines and trains, and no Michael Severance was found in the passenger manifests. She then started to worry, and feared for the worst. That evening, Leslie arrived home from work at 6 p.m. and was informed by Brinda that Michael was missing. He immediately called Wendi, who told him that she'd left Michael in the house and had taken the kids in his truck to go visit her parents. When she came back, Michael was nowhere to be found. Leslie immediately go suspicious because Michael's truck was supposed to be in the shop for maintenance, and his son loved his truck too much to forget to take it in.

After the phone call, Wendi and Lloyd went to the San Angelo Police Department to file a missing persons report. Office Lucien Thomas informed her that investigators would drop by the clinic the next morning. Wendi then called the Air Force and reported that Staff Sergeant Michael Severance was missing. On Monday morning, Detective Dennis McGuire of the San Angelo Police Department arrived at the clinic. He found Marshall and his sister at the premise, the clinic fully functional despite Wendi's "loss." At the time, Marshall was a Game Warden in Zapata, four hundred miles from San Angelo.

Detective McGuire requested permission to look around. As he walked through the facility, he noted a knife with a blue handle, a computer, and the drugs present in the clinic. He found Michael's Ford pick-up truck in the parking lot, with his cell phone inside the cab. He spoke to Wendi, who informed him that her husband was on leave until January 24, and that he had spoken about going AWOL and hiding out in Canada. When Frank Severance called his brother's cell, an unidentified policeman answered and stated, "We'll probably find him shacked up somewhere with a whore." The Severance family quickly lost hope in the San Angelo Police Department's investigation. Leslie then called Michael's commanding officer, Captain Bill Walker, who explained that they had no cause to investigate until Michael was declared AWOL on January 24.

On January 26, Wendi logged into her computer and searched for details about decomposition of bodies in the water. She discovered than in cold water, the body would rise to the surface within two to three weeks. She immediately formulated a plan to prevent the discovery of Michael's body. She took her blue-handled boning knife, a few spare parts from the barn and then went to the 7777 Ranch's dump pile to find more items to weigh down the body. At the stock tank, she saw that Michael's body had started to surface, and was delighted to have found it before anyone else. She took a boat to the middle of the pond, and using a paddle, guided Michael's body to the bank. She then stabbed him 41 times to make it easy for the air trapped in his body to escape. She then used yellow braided rope and plastic zip ties to fasten the other heavy items to the body. In the process, some of the items fell into the mud. She then guided the boat to the smaller side of the stock tank and threw the body into the water. She watched until it sank, and was satisfied by her accomplishment. She then got back into her car and drove home.

March 5, 2005

Marshall, Lloyd, Judy, and Tristan were just about to have dinner when the phone rang. It was Wendi, and she claimed that someone was chasing her and she was at Grape Creek Cemetery. Marshall took his pistol and went to find his sister. When he arrived, he was a 2001 red Camaro first, and then Wendi standing by their grandfather's grave. When he asked about who was chasing her, she admitted that she had lied. However, she had something she needed to get off her chest and that she wanted to wait until their parent got there. Marshall couldn't wait, and insisted that she tell him what was wrong. She stated, "I didn't kill Mike, but, you know, I did find him dead, and I moved his body to the tank." She then claimed that she thought one of her family members had killed him and was just trying to protect them. Lloyd and Judy pulled up into the cemetery, and Wendi repeated the story to her parents. At the time, Michael's young infant was in the Camaro.

Marshall, a law enforcement officer, decided to do the right thing. He called the San Angelo Police Department and asked for Detective Dennis McGuire. Little did he know that the detective and Sergeant Dave Jones of the Texas Department of Public Safety were in the vicinity. In February, the detectives and members of the Air Force Office of Special Investigation had installed trackers in Wendi's and Judy's cars, as they had suspected that the Davidsons were not forthcoming with their story about Michael's disappearance. At the same time, Officer Bill Mabe was at the 7777 Ranch gate, securing the scene.

That night at 11.30 p.m., Judy was arrested on charges of tampering with evidence, a third-degree felony. The judge who officiated her wedding, Judge Eddie Howard, signed Wendi's arrest warrant and set the bong for $500,000. Wendi was then transferred to the Tom Green County Jail and was put on suicide watch.

Trial and Sentencing

The investigation into Michael's cause of death took a long while to bear fruit. On April 8 2005, Texas Ranger Shawn Palmer contacted Dr. Sridhar Natarajan at the Lubbock County Medical Examiner's Office. After the long wait, Michael's toxicology report was back. The lab had found Phenobarbital and high levels of pentobarbital in Michael Severance's cavity fluid, gastric content, and tissues taken from the liver. To Palmer, Michael's cause of death was clear. Wendi was subsequently arrested and charged with murder.

Her defense team consisted of Fred C. Brigman III, Christi Manning, and Melvin Gray. Wendi's trial date was slated for March 20, 2006. However, her attorneys repeatedly asked for continuances, and her hearing finally started on October 16 2006. Wendi's lawyers filed a motion for the suppression of the evidence recovered through the use of the trackers. However, the court denied that request, and the evidence was admitted. Since there whole defense was based on suppressing the tracker evidence, it became clear that they were losing the case. Wendi was therefore advised to plead "no contest," and was assured that she would face minimal jail time, or none. Wendi pleaded "no contest" and was sentenced to 25 years on the murder conviction, and 10 years each on the two tampering charges, to be served concurrently. She would qualify for parole after 13 years.

On 10 May 2019, the Texas Board of Pardons and Parole voted to reject Wendi's parole request. She is next eligible for parole in 2024.

JASMINE RICHARDSON

On the South Saskatchewan River in Alberta, Canada is a town called Medicine Hat. With a population of just over 60,000 it is filled with little communities where everybody knows everybody. With a relatively low crime rate and virtually none of those crimes involving homicide it's the perfect place to raise a family in a safe environment, or at least it would seem that way I should I say. The security offered by Medicine Hat was greatly diminished when the entire town was shaken to its core in April of 2006.

On April 23, 2006 the community was rocked to its very foundation with the discovery of a gruesome triple homicide. An entire family was found stabbed to death in their home that day. The bodies were discovered by the 8 year old boy's best friend when he arrived at the house to get his friend to come out and play. When cops were notified and an investigation began the scene revealed was one of the worst scenes in Canadian history. Debra Richardson, 48 and her husband Marc, 42 were found in the basement with multiple stab wounds covering their bodies and upon further investigation their son 8 year old Jacob was found also stabbed to death with his throat slit in his bed upstairs. Such a horrific scene was left behind that the police responding would be affected long after the investigation. It didn't take police long to realize that family photos around the home depicted a family of 4 instead of 3. The 12 year old daughter Jasmine was missing. Immediately police were concerned that they had a kidnapping on their hands. The sweet angelic looking daughter in the photos must have been victimized by the monster that did this to her family as well. However, the sweet loving family photos that the police encountered depicting a 12 year old girl were not the reality where Jasmine was concerned. Jasmine had started acting and dressing differently. She had new friends, she was getting in trouble and going off to wild parties and she had a 23 year old boyfriend that her parents detested here being with. That boyfriend was into drugs, drinking, and dark things like werewolves, vampires, and the Goth culture. In fact that boyfriend even claimed to be a werewolf himself and reportedly professed to liking the taste of blood. Jasmine Richardson was not missing because she had been kidnapped rather she was missing because she was responsible. It would be later discovered that Jasmine and her 23 year old boyfriend, Jeremy Steinke had committed the murders themselves and had gone on the run.

Background

Once upon a time Jasmine Richardson was the sweet little girl depicted in the family photos around the Richardson house. Once upon a time the family was the perfect poster family for suburban bliss but something went wrong. Jasmine became interested in the Goth culture as well as the Wiccan religion. With this interest came a dark side to the little girl.

At 12 the little girl looked much older; perhaps 15 or 16 and she even claimed to be that old on social media. Soon she had the attention of local man Jeremy Steinke. Jasmine and Jeremy fell into a dangerous relationship. They idolized a life of negativity. They dressed in dark fantasy type clothing and they frequented sites on the internet like vampire freaks, a social media site for teens that love all things vampire. In fact Jeremy himself claimed to love the taste of blood and that he was a 300 year old werewolf. Jeremy had more practice at the twisted lifestyle that they both began to lead than Jasmine did but he was also weakened by a controlling effect that Jasmine had on him. Jasmine knew how to manipulate Jeremy. In many ways this seemed to spell love for Jeremy; he had found a girl that he would do anything for. In Jasmine's case Jeremy was an adult that she could control. She might have to live under what felt like the tyranny of her parents and she might have to go by the rules at the strict Catholic school that she attended but with Jeremy she had the say so. She could only wish for something and Jeremy was there to try to make her wishes come true. This might all sound like the musings of a warped but innocent mind, a reality created by dissatisfied kids looking to feel like they have more control over their lives but Jasmine and Jeremy took things much farther than most kids would dare to go. Just like any good loving parents the Richardsons became alarmed when they learned of the changes in their daughter's lifestyle. The most alarming thing to Jasmine's parents was Jeremy. No parent is going to be comfortable with their 12 year old little girl being in a relationship with a 23 year old man. More alarmingly their relationship was sexual as well. Jasmine may have looked much older but she still had the mind and body of a 12 year old girl chronologically speaking.

When Jasmine told Jeremy online that she had a plan to kill her family he hopped on board. They wrote instant messages to each other discussing the killing of Jasmine's family. Below are the exact words they typed to each other in a snippet of their conversation.

Jasmine: "I have this plan. It begins with me killing them and ends with me living with you."

Jeremy: "I love your plan but we need to get a little more creative with like details and stuff."

Who knows now if either of them were truly serious about committing the murders in the beginning but in the end Jeremy got pumped up watching the movie *Natural Born Killers,* got drunk, did some lines of cocaine and then he was ready to help his beloved carry out her request to alleviate herself of her bothersome parents. All it took was a set of loving protective parents trying to protect their 12 year old daughter from the psychological and perhaps even physical damage that would come from having a sexual relationship with a 23 year old man and Jasmine and Jeremy were all too ready to put an end to the two nuisances trying to keep them apart.

On the night of April 22nd Jeremy watched *Natural Born Killers* with his friends, did some drinking and drugs and then he was ready. He would do anything to make Jasmine happy. Despite her young age and the considerable age gap between the two Jasmine knew how to manipulate Jeremy. Jeremy snuck into the basement of The Richardson's split level home and waited. Thinking she heard noises Debra Richardson, already in her night gown, went down to investigate. She couldn't have been prepared for what awaited her. As soon as Debra flipped on the light switch Jeremy attacked her stabbing her 12 times before killing her. Debra's husband Marc was close behind after hearing the commotion and armed with a screwdriver. However, in the end his screwdriver was no match for Jeremy's knife. Later Jeremy would tell an undercover police officer that he was worried Marc would get the better of him and that Marc nearly succeeded in defending himself with that screwdriver. No matter the fight Marc put up the scene ended up with him on the floor still in a defensive stance, dead with 24 stab wounds. Later Jeremy would say that Marc asked 'why' just before he died and Jeremy replied, 'it's what your daughter wanted.'

After killing Marc and Debra Jeremy headed upstairs leaving a trail of blood in his wake. Upstairs Jasmine was trying to calm her little brother down. At this point Jeremy and Jasmine's stories are not the same. Both of them say it was the other that actually killed the little boy. I suppose we will never know the truth nevertheless young Jacob was found in his bed with stab wounds in his body and his throat slit side to side. Jasmine and Jeremy left the scene and reportedly went back to a friend's apartment to have sex after obliterating Jasmine's entire family. They were the outlaw lovers that they had dreamed of being bound together even more so by the horrific blood bath they had just caused. The two went on the run but they didn't make it far. After a search of Jasmine's school locker a graphic picture surfaced of a girl's whole family burning in a fire while she laughs and escapes with her boyfriend. When police saw this drawing they went from searching for Jasmine as a victim to searching for her as a suspect.

Jasmine and Jeremy were apprehended in Saskatchewan the very next day after the bodies of her family were discovered. The pair were reportedly laughing and joking around with friends about the murders only one day after they had taken place.

Unfathomable Murder

The Richardsons were the picturesque family living in a picturesque neighborhood. Ross Glen, the community where the Richardsons lived, was a middle class neighborhood full of working class families. Their neighbors on one side were Sara and her six year old son Gareth, Jacob's best friend, and their neighbors on the other side were Phyllis and Vernon Gehring. The Gehrings were an elderly couple that liked to garden and look after their dog, a shi tzu Bishon mix. Often the scene would be that Gareth and Jacob could be found playing in the backyard as children do and the Gehrings would delight in tossing balls back over the fence when they strayed a bit too far. The Gehrings felt like Jacob kept them young. They admittedly didn't know much about the daughter. Just the night before that fateful afternoon when the bodies were found Marc Richardson had grilled hot dogs in the backyard for the boys while the Gehring's dog played with the Richardson family's dog through the fence. Everything seemed perfect in that sleepy little neighborhood until that fateful afternoon on April 23rd when Gareth went looking for his best friend.

It was about 1pm and Sara and Gareth had been at Sara's mom's house but Gareth had been asking to play with Jacob all morning. When Gareth could not get anyone to answer the phone at the Richardson residence Sara told him that they could go to the movies. Gareth was still bummed out about not getting to see Jacob and when he and his mom returned home before heading to the movies he darted over to the Richardson's after seeing that Marc's white pickup truck was in the driveway. Gareth knocked on the door but there was no answer, as a curious little boy might he began peering into the basement windows of the split level home. When he saw lifeless bodies and a basement covered in blood he ran back to his mom to tell her what he'd seen. Although Gareth wasn't usually the type of boy to make up stories the things he was saying to Sara just didn't make sense. As she followed him over to the neighbor's house she warned him that he had better not be lying. Sadly Gareth was not lying. When she peered through the same windows that Gareth had Sara saw a horrible scene in front of her. She was afraid that the intruder that had done this was still around, maybe he was even in her house waiting for her and Gareth. She called her mom and her mom told her she had to call 911. Sara's mom and the police headed to the scene. What would unfold at that crime scene would haunt police officers that investigated for years to come. Some of the officers involved were touched so much by young Jacob's defiled body that they broke down on the stand months later when they had to talk about it.

The police came in thinking that they might have an intruder still lurking about the property. They entered with caution. What they saw was unfathomable. There were the bodies of a man and woman in the basement both covered in blood. The woman, Debra Richardson was slumped in the floor with her night gown hiked up exposing the fact that all she had been wearing when she was attacked was that night gown. There was blood all over her and a pool of blood all around her. The little black family dog was standing beside her. Perhaps he felt that he needed to protect her but sadly it was too late for that. Across the basement slumped against a wall was Marc Richardson. His hands were straight out as though he were trying to defend himself. He was frozen by rigor mortis in a defensive state that did nothing for his defense in the end. Marc was wearing only black boxer shorts and a screwdriver was lying beside him. He, too, was riddled with stab wounds. The entire basement was covered in splatters of blood, there had been a real struggle between the Richardsons and their assailant. Upon further investigation of the house the police came across their worst nightmare. The first bedroom was empty but the next bedroom they came to was Jacob's. Jacob was lying in his bed. Police had hope for a moment that the boy was still alive but when they approached they were greeted with the worst. Jacob was in his bed with his throat slashed and stab wounds littering his body as well. There was blood all over his room including many of his toys. A toy light saber was lying in his floor; a useless object against the onslaught of the knife that had ended his life. In the master bedroom the comforter was thrown back as though the bed's occupants had left in a hurry. There was a pillow thrown awkwardly in the floor. Police wondered with horror if the boy had heard his parents being attacked before the assailant ever made it upstairs to him and clutched the pillow trying to find some comfort in the act. As they made another sweep of the house the police noticed that there were four members of the Richardson family instead of three. Instantly everyone's heart sank. A family photo depicted a sweet smiling 12 year old girl and she was nowhere to be found. Police searched that house several times over for either the body of the little girl or perhaps the girl hiding somewhere too afraid to come out after the horrible things she had witnessed but in the end they had to admit defeat, the fourth member of the Richardson family was nowhere to be seen. On the plus side her body wasn't there slain with the rest of her family but the police had to think the worst. The most logical thought was that she may have been kidnapped by whoever did this to her family. And even if she was safe, perhaps spending the night at a friend's house she would still have to deal with the tragic news that she had no family left, that her family had all been brutally attacked and killed. Hearts went out for the girl and for the family she had lost. No one wanted to be left breaking that news to a 12 year old.

The hunt for Jasmine Richardson began, or actually continued, as her parents had reported that she was missing before the terrible crime had ever even taken place. Where was Jasmine? Safe, but oblivious to the fact that this terrible thing had happened to her parents? Scared alone and possibly seriously injured in the hands of the monster that did this to her family? No one could say. As part of the investigation police visited Jasmine's school and got permission to look inside her locker. They were looking for any kind of evidence that would lead them to Jasmine whatsoever but what they found was truly a shocking discovery. When the police searched Jasmine's locker they found a hand drawn picture depicting a horrible scene. In the picture a girl's family burns to death after she puts gasoline in the sprinklers while they have a family picnic. The stick figure girl in the drawing laughs as her family burns and she escapes in her boyfriend's pickup truck. This drawing shifted suspicions entirely and Jasmine Richardson went from being searched for as a victim to being searched for as a suspect in the murder of her parents and her little brother. Consequently it didn't take the police long to track Jasmine and Jeremy down. The pair were said to be joking around with friends about the murders even at the time of apprehension. They were found at a high school in Saskatchewan only about 60 miles from Medicine Hat.

Both Jasmine and Jeremy were jailed and both were convicted. Because of Jasmine's young age at the time under Canadian law she had to be referred to as JR instead of her name. She also was protected from being tried as an adult. Although she got the maximum sentence for a child her age that sentence was only 10 years and under the conditions the time she had already spent in jail counted toward her 10 years. She ended up being imprisoned under the conditions of 4 years locked up undergoing rehabilitation and 4.5 years under very close supervision in the community. Jeremy, on the other hand, was 23 years old at the time of the murders. He was found guilty of three counts of first degree murder and sentenced to three life sentences to be served consecutively. An undercover officer rode with Jeremy while he was being transported from one facility to the other. In the conversation the two had together Jeremy expressed that he loved Jasmine more than anything and that the kind of thing he did was the kind of thing that truly expressed that love. He admitted to everything he did in such a straight forward way that it seemed he did not even grasp the gravity of the situation. He even shared his plans to marry Jasmine when they were both able to get out of prison. On murderpedia.org you can actually read the transcript of the conversation that Jeremy had with the undercover officer that he believed to be another prison being transported along with him. Steinke will be eligible for parole after 25 years.

Some of the residents of Medicine Hat were actually outraged with the outcome of the trial. They didn't think that justice would be served with Jasmine getting away with such little time. Wayne Chopek is one such resident that has spoken out about his outrage. Wayne was a friend of the family and he is disgusted at the fact that Jasmine would go free after a short ten years. However, the law remains the law and in Canada the government believes that children as young as Jasmine was at the time of the murders need to be rehabilitated rather than being locked up and having the key thrown away. They believe that such young lives have more potential value than to doom them to the rest of their lives behind bars.

Life After Murder

After Jasmine and Jeremy were arrested and jailed they still held onto the flame that was recklessly burning before the murders. They were not able to have any contact with one another except for letter writing so they wrote back and forth. This is how Jeremy came to ask Jasmine to marry him and she said yes. Below is an excerpt of the letters passed between the two when Jeremy popped the question.

Jeremy: "Without you this life isn't worth living... U said you want to get engaged? Then here's a Q...Will U marry me? If so then it is a verbal agreement!"

Jasmine: "Ahahaha! I never thought I'd find myself hystericaly laughing in a holding cell in these kinds of circumstances...or ever really. But still! ahaha you make me so happy! Yes! Yes! I will, I would love to... "

Interestingly enough as bright as that flame might have been it eventually flickered out. Although they professed the deepest of bonds neither of the two would admit to actually being the one to Kill Jacob. Both blamed the other. This was one of the deciding factors that actually showed that there were holes in the loving couple's relationship. The two broke up in jail. After incarceration the relationship that had been important enough to kill for dwindled until it was no more.

Perhaps free of any attachment to Jeremy Steinke Jasmine could truly rehabilitate. Jasmine underwent psychiatric evaluations and was determined to be suffering from oppositional defiance disorder as well as conduct disorder. When she first started therapy she was determined to suffer from dependency issues, anxiety and depression. As well as all this she was prone to immature problem solving and wishful fantasies. All this is a lot to bog down a 12 year old but was it enough of a load to excuse the execution of the murder of her entire family? Many say no, some say yes. At any rate it is indeed enough to at least explain some of her behaviors. Once in therapy Jasmine began making progress toward rehabilitation though in the beginning her details of how things played out her a bit skewed to reality. By 2010 Jasmine was making significant progress in her rehabilitation and had professed to be sorry for the crimes she committed. As the terms of her sentencing were laid out she got credit on her sentence for the time she spent in jail awaiting trial and then after 4 years of incarceration she was deemed fit enough to go into the community under very close supervision for 4.5 years. During that time Jasmine was shown to exhibit exemplary behavior as well as being a straight A student. Jasmine was admitted to Calgary University where she continued to earn really high grades. This year, 2016, in May Jasmine became a completely free woman. The courts have no reason to think that she is a danger to society any longer. It's been a decade and she has been through extensive amounts of therapy and shown nothing but progress in that entire time.

A very interesting thing to look at here is the chemistry between Jasmine and Jeremy. One asks themselves, was the combination just toxic? Would either of them been capable of doing something like this on their own? It seems that the pairing of the two and the dependency that both of them exhibited for the other was actual such an explosive combination that it pushed them over the edge just enough to create the perfect circumstance for this to happen. Jasmine has said that she wasn't really being serious when she would send Jeremy messages saying that she had a plan to kill her parents and live with him. That she didn't really mean to go through with it when she joked about murdering her family or made drawings depicting their deaths. But she felt those feelings and she told Jeremy. Steinke just happened to be easily manipulated, a regular user of multiple drugs, and even believed himself to be a 300 year old werewolf. Jeremy and Jasmine both took the dark Goth culture they lived within to the extreme. They exchanged vials of blood and Jeremy wore one around his neck. When the two were faced with Jasmine's parents making them unable to see one another dark fantasies were transformed into evil realities. Perhaps the fantasies that both harbored were purely fantasies until the tension kept rising and rising and the two kept feeding off of each other until the combination of each of their dark thoughts breathed life into the other. In the end it doesn't really matter to ask if either would have been capable of the atrocity on their own because it wasn't the case that they were on their own. They were bound together by an obsessive unhealthy love and the obsessive unhealthy thoughts in both their heads took form in reality. The result was unspeakable horror.

That late April day three lives were lost much too soon and in such a violent way that it is nearly unthinkable. That alone is enough to make this tragedy stand out forever in history but that's not all that was lost. Little Gareth will never be the same. Though he is a successful high schooler now the memory of those bodies and the memory of the loss of his best friend will always be with him. And of course Jasmine Richardson and Jeremy Steinke's lives will forever be changed and affected. Jeremy will most likely spend his entire life in jail having had only 23 short years of freedom. Parole will be an unlikely event. Even though Jasmine has improved and rehabilitated, even if she successfully integrates back into society, she will forever have this as a part of her past. She will also forever have people that look at her as a monster. Her story is known all over the world. Jasmine is the youngest person in Canada to have ever committed such a heinous crime. It is a question to ponder as to whether Jasmine has forgiven herself or if she is forever haunted by the monster that she perhaps did not even know lurked inside her. Perhaps even scarier to think of is the possibility that she really could live without being constantly haunted by the crime. Is there any amount of rehabilitation that should erase that guilt? And then one has to consider Jeremy. Has he come to terms with the events? Is he sorry for his crimes? Will a life in prison in any way begin to repay his debt for those three lives that he so brutally extinguished?

Life in Medicine Hat continues on. It is still a relatively safe place to live. Medicine Hat is still a relatively small tight knit place filled with working class suburbs. There are still nice neighborhoods that feel safe the way that Ross Glen did before tragedy came to town but no one will forget what could happen no matter how nice or normal a family might seem they will know that a tragedy like this could happen to any family because it already has.

CHILD KILLER MANLING WILLIAMS

CRYSTAL STONE

Manling Williams was born in 1979 as Manling Tsang. She tended to go by the nickname "Ling" while growing up. As a child, she was diagnosed with various learning disabilities and experienced many challenges academically while in school. Williams was the result of an unwanted pregnancy between her two parents, and she was nearly aborted. Ultimately, she was born into a family that didn't want her, and they treated her as such throughout her childhood with copious amounts of verbal and physical abuse.

In her childhood, Williams struggled to make friends. At one point when she was growing up, she stole money from her parents in order to buy friends at school, as she couldn't make them no matter how hard she tried. She did not do well socially. That incident resulted in a public scolding that was so severe and inappropriate that Child Protective Services became involved. While her mother was chastising her in front of her peers, she slapped her face repeatedly. Although Child Protective Services was called, nothing tangible came of it, and the case was closed. Manling remained with her parents and her sister for the remainder of her childhood and into her early adulthood.

Many would later testify that Manling's parents repeatedly called her stupid due to her lack of success in school, and that physical abuse went on as well. In one incident, a foreign exchange student who was living with the family recalled that her father slapped her face four or five times when she was suspected of stealing money from a friend. Manling ran to her room in tears.

In 1999, Neal Williams met and fell in love with his 20-year-old coworker at Subway, Manling. "He thought she was beautiful," Neal's mom, Jan Williams, later said in a statement to reporters. "He liked that he could talk to her about a lot of things." Neal was considered to be affable and intelligent. He was well-liked, and liked to watch Star Wars and quote Monty Python. He was considered to be very bright and was particularly close with his mom, Jan, and his older sister, Mala.

Shortly after they began dating, Manling became illegitimately pregnant with Neal's child. On July 26, 2000, Neal and Manling's had a baby boy, whom they named Devon. Devon was described by his grandmother Jan as silly, sociable, and tolerant. He wished to study monkeys when he grew up and attend Whittier College, which is where his grandmother worked. Everyone loved Devon. A family friend had chosen to have him as the ring bearer in her wedding. "He couldn't stand to see someone upset or treated unfairly," the friend recalled. If he saw someone being treated unfairly, or if he saw that someone felt sad or was upset, he took steps to fix it, even at a young age.

Jan Williams recalled one painful memory of Devon having some normal anxiety about nighttime and being afraid of the dark, a memory which stings his grandmother to this day. The two were singing a nighttime song about a dragon. Devon expressed concern because the song alluded to little boys who died in their beds. "I told him he was safe in his bed, and he wasn't," his grandmother later said sadly.

In 2001, Manling and baby Devon were in the car with Judy, Neal's mom. Manling officially asked Judy for permission to marry his son. "Only if you promise not to hurt him," she replied lightly, and the pair laughed, having no idea of knowing what lay ahead.

Having had a child out of wedlock did nothing to improve Williams' ongoing tumultuous relationship with her parents. She was forced to move out of their home and temporarily lived with friends and her mother-in-law, Jan Williams. Neal and Manling eventually became engaged, got married at a courthouse, and later had a big wedding at a Taiwanese church. The trio then moved into a condo in Rowling Heights in Los Angeles county, California, where they would live until everything ended. The neighborhood was cozy and safe, and the neighbors were friendly.

Manling and Neal's second son, Ian, was born in the Fall of 2003. Ian liked to pester his older brother, and "threw himself into life with great abandon," according to his grandmother's recollections. He would do things like get his head stuck between the railings on the banister, build a ladder out of chairs and climb to the top, and knock down whatever structure Devon had just created. He also hated any sort of nickname or pet name, and insisted vehemently, "My name is IAN!"

A few years went by where, by all appearances, Manling, Neal, Devon, and Ian were a happy and regular family. At this time, Williams worked at Marie Callender's as a waitress, while Neal did a lot of computer work from home. In the months leading up to the incident, Manling had connected with an old friend named John Gregory via MySpace, and subsequently began an affair with him. This was a man that she had had an attraction, or rather an infatuation, for since the days of high school. Almost immediately after their affair began, Gregory began to pressure Manling to get a divorce and ended up breaking things off with her shortly after, while promising that they could get back together if she ended up terminating her marriage. Meanwhile, Williams had grown tired of being a mother and a wife, and was feeling very distant from her children.

Beginning in June of 2007, Manling began to randomly tell her friends that she was having dreams of Neal smothering their sons and then killing himself. No one made much of these comments, aside from thinking that they were disturbing and unfortunate. Williams and her husband had been having significant marital problems, often resulting in profanity-laced arguments and slamming doors that could be heard by neighbors outside of their home. The home they lived in was filled with piles of clothes and trash, with unwashed dishes and more trash on the kitchen counters, and was chronically very unkempt. However, despite their marital difficulties, Neal was by all accounts an excellent father. He enjoyed reading to his children, playing catch with them, and taking them to baseball games.

On August 7, 2007, Maling smothered her two young sons with a pillow in their bunk bed, and slashed her husband to death with a sword in the family's condominium. With regard to her children, Ian was in the bottom bunk with a teddy bear blanket, and Devon was in the top bunk, under a Spongebob blanket. Her husband Neal was 27 years old at the time, the same age as Manling. Devon was age seven, and Ian, age three. Autopsy results would show that the boys had died within two hours after eating their last meal, which was pineapple pizza delivered to the home at 8:20 pm. Computer records showed that after she smothered them, Manling left the boys dead in their beds and checked her boyfriend's MySpace page. She then went out with friends to dinner to TGIFridays. A friend who was at dinner with her would later testify that Williams was behaving normally, and that Williams often spoke lovingly of her children. Four days prior to the killings, on August 3, Williams had sent her lover a single red rose, with the message "thinking of you." She had signed it as being from a secret admirer.

Neal was asleep in bed when Mailing returned home. Manling retrieved and used a katana sword that had been given to Neal by his mother, as he was a sword collector.The knife had a 10-inch handle, a 20-inch blade, and was incredibly sharp. While he was sleeping, she stabbed him in the chest. Neal did not die in the bed, which indicated that he had gotten up tried to run in an attempt to escape.

The autopsy report would show that Neal's hands were mangled as he tried to fend off the attack, and he had a giant "X" slashed on his torso. He lost the tips of two fingers and broke several other fingers attempting to defend himself. He had 22 wounds on his hands alone. He only made it as far as the top of the stairs, which was a short distance from their bedroom, and the katana was found near his body. Neal was stabbed and slashed 97 times total in the attack. In his final moments, he begged Williams for help, a call which was left unheeded. He suffered a fatal wound when he was initially stabbed through the heart, damaging his right ventricle and his aorta, which takes blood to the brain. This was actually the first strike from the katana, but it wasn't an immediately fatal one. Autopsy results showed that both of his lungs were punctured and filled with blood (500 cubic centimeters in the right lung, and 200 cubic centimeters in the left). In addition, he suffered a wound through his back that went "through and through" and departed his body via his neck, damaging his thyroid gland in the process. One of the other most damaging wounds went through his small intestine. In addition, a "chopping" type of wound was located on the back of his neck that fractured his skull and caused bleeding in the brain. Neal's mother would end up having chronic, recurrent nightmares of his nearly severed hands after learning about them in trial. Deputy Tim Bryant later testified that he nearly fell when he stepped over Neal, because there was so much blood that had saturated the carpet around him.

Immediately following the murder, Manling typed a fake suicide note on Neal's behalf stating that Neal had killed the children and then himself. The letter stated that Neal was having an affair and hinted at killing the children before committing suicide. "Please for give [sic] me for being a coward and not being there for you," Manling wrote under the guise of Neal's voice. She posted the note on MySpace. She disposed of all bloody clothing in a dumpster a fair distance from their home. These clothes were later recovered and were confirmed to have Neal's blood on them. Then she returned home and ran outside, screaming to neighbors at 7:30 am that someone had killed her family.

Several neighbors ran to assist and after speaking to Manling, went into the house before the police arrived, not understanding what they would find. In court, one neighbor would describe seeing Neal at the top of the stairs. "I seen Neal laying there, stabbed up. I looked into his eyes and blood was just dripping and dripping." This same neighbor found the little boys and described through tears what he found while on the stand. "I shook the little blanket but there was no movement, nothing, no movement."

Manling's account of what had happened became contradictory almost immediately. Upon calling her neighbors over at 7:30 am via her frantic screaming, she told them she had gone out for Red Bull and cigarettes and had returned to find the crime scene. She then told investigators that she had gone for a drive because she couldn't sleep, then later stated that she had gone grocery shopping (though she was wearing boxer shorts, smelled of alcohol, and was barefoot when her neighbors saw her, suggesting that she hadn't recently gone anywhere).

When Neal's mother, Jan Williams, heard the news, she got a ride to the sheriff's station right away, where she met with Manling's parents. The trio hugged and cried as they waited for more news. They waited for Manling to come out after her interview with police. However, Manling was never released, and soon, a terrible realizations began to set in.

For several hours, while being interviewed by investigators following the discovery of the bodies, Manling feigned sadness, grief and bewilderment on camera. She said things like, "Does anyone know if my husband is okay? I want my babies. Please let them be okay." Only after investigators found a bloody cigarette box in her car and confronted her did Williams confess to the crimes. Blood was found in a spot on her bra that matched where Neal's blood was found on the bloody shirt that was thrown into the dumpster. Neal's blood was also found on her feet. After her confession, she was arrested on three counts of homicide one day after the murders, on August 8, 2007.

Detective Donald Walls recalled that Manling was arrogant in her interviews, that she was relaxed as if they were having a normal lunchtime conversation, and that she made jokes about the TV show CSI. The Williams' neighbors in the 18200 block of Camino Bello in Rowland Heights, California, were first shocked and then horrified as police spread crime scene tape around their property and began carrying out multiple bins of evidence. One piece of evidence that was later shown in court was a dictionary that had a page marked by having a knife placed inside. On this page was the definition of the word "marriage." In the yard lay discarded equipment: a football, a bat, and a plastic pitching machine.

Manling originally stated in her confession that Neil had "passed out drunk" the night of the killings, but toxicology reports later showed that he did not have drugs or alcohol in his system. He was sober when he died. After Manling's arrest, it took more than a year for the first preliminary hearing to take place due to repeated delays and postponements. This process was very hard on the victim's family. Neal's mother and sister were particularly open with reporters throughout the process as they waited for the trial process to begin.

With the verdict in, the next part of the legal process was the penalty phase, in which jurors would recommend whether Manling should receive life in prison or the death penalty as her sentence. Manling's defense attorneys, Tom Althaus and Haydeh Takasugi, argued that Manling should receive a life sentence and not the death penalty, arguing that the murders were not calculated, but rather "a sudden mistake," and that Manling was in a state of "extreme emotional and mental disturbance" when the killings occurred. They noted that "it was clear that the family unit was unraveling." However, as Los Angeles County Deputy District Attorneys Stacy Okun-Wiese and Pak Kouch pointed out, Williams had put on latex gloves prior to killing her husband, indicating that the killing could not be correctly defined as "spur of the moment." The defense attempted to paint Manling as a socially awkward loner who was mentally unstable and who was overburdened by cultural expectations.

The defense also argued that Williams had a difficult upbringing, and that her life was defined by pain, heartbreak, and "diminished dreams." They noted that she was reputed to be a very charitable person prior to the killings, that she was previously well known for lovin her husband and children (a contradictory assertion to several neighborhood eyewitnesses), and that she had no history of violence. A few additional witnesses continued to contradict this picture, however, such as one of her neighbors, who indicated that Manling rarely said more than hello, and that "she would just stand outside her house, smoking and smoking." The defense focused almost solely on the upbringing and abuse Williams experienced at the hands of her mother. Manling's father, Kai Tai Tsang, while on the stand, appealed directly to Neal's mother and apologized. "I feel really sorry. Please forgive me. As a father, I didn't do good. That is why it happened. I am sorry."

Williams' former lover, John Gregory, testified that after Manling contacted him on MySpace in June of 2007, the two went to dinner with two other people from their high school, during which time Manling discussed that she wasn't happy at home or in her relationship. In July of 2007, Manling went to see Gregory in Santa Barbara for a weekend, and the two had an affair. According to his testimony, Gregory ended the affair a few days later. He reported that Manling seemed "normal" throughout the affair and also upon breaking up. Gregory had initially denied the affair to investigators, but later came clean. "I felt really uncomfortable and slightly responsible that I contributed to her emotional state," he said. Manling's friend Melaney Ramirez also testified with regard to Williams' emotional state, saying that according to previous conversations they had had, Manling felt forced into marriage because she accidentally became pregnant. Another friend, Jaclyn Bailey, testified that Manling and Neal would fight "almost every day," and that the fights would often escalate to screaming. Bailey also stated that she had lived with the Williams for three months, and that she was "beyond shocked" because she always thought Williams loved her children, even if there were struggles in the marriage.

With regard to whether or not the killings were premeditated, testimony during Williams' trial indicated that the suffocation method of using a pillow by which she killed her first child took five to 10 minutes, which was ample time for Williams to consider her actions. However, she then went on to kill her second child in precisely the same way. This in additional to wearing the latex gloves and mentioning the manner of death to friends up to two months prior to the killings, made it difficult for the defense to form a solid argument about the killings being spur of the moment.

Neal's mother was present during the trial and was often seen taking notes on what was being presented in an almost clinical manner. However, one week into the trial, she broke down as blood spatter pictures were being shown to the jury, and she saw one of her grandson's favorite stuffed animals (a dragon that her grandsons had named Puff) in the background of the photo. She was also forced to watch a clip of Manling calmly telling a detective what Neal's last words were ("Help me").

Mangling went to trial in November of 2010, and the trial took approximately six weeks. A jury, after deliberating for eight hours, convicted Manling of three counts of first-degree murder, along with the special allegations of using weapons and lying in wait. The jury of six men and six women was unable to agree, with a vote of 8-4, on whether life in prison or the death penalty was a more appropriate punishment, so the decision was given to a second jury. The second jury recommended in 2011 that Williams be put to death.

There was much controversy around the sequence of the two juries who were tasked with deciding the outcome for Williams. Manling's sister, Shun Ling Tsang, urged the judge to consider life without parole instead of the death penalty rather than retrying the penalty phase after the first hung jury. She had given testimony during the trial that her sister's behavior had changed in the months leading up to the murders, and that she would often call her sister in the middle of the night "just to talk," which was new and unusual behavior. She argued that the prosecution's continued pursuit of the death penalty was "ego driven" and "politically motivated." After the first jury was unable to come to a decision, members of both families asserted that they would prefer to see a life sentence with no possibility of parole, and no possibility of appeal. The defense again appealed for life in prison over the death penalty, emphasizing Manling's lack of previous violence, as well as her difficult upbringing. However, the prosecution decided to re-try the penalty phase, which resulted in the death penalty. The second penalty phase of the trial began on April 18, 2011. Prosecuting attorney Stacy Okun-Wiese scoffed at the defense's attempt to pin the murders on Manling's childhood, stating "When did it become okay in our society to commit three heinous crimes, kill your children and your husband, and blame it on your mom?"

Williams was sentenced to death on January 8, 2012 for the murders of her family per the jury's recommendation. "It is the order of the court that you should suffer the penalty of death," Judge Robert Martinez said to Manling. She was 32 years old at the time of her sentencing. Manling, dressed in an orange prison jumper with glasses on, sat in handcuffs and stared down at the table during the duration of the sentencing, then sobbed and visibly shook after the support was read. She leaned on her defense attorney, Haydeh Takasugi, who openly cared about Williams on a personal level, and who was deeply invested in the case. Manling was often seen in court that way - head down, eyes down, unable to look the world in the face.

Neal's mother, Jan Williams, expressed gratitude that the trial was finally over, citing the "terrible" impact the events had had on everyone involved, including the Tsang family. She has stated "This is their tragedy, too. I don't blame them for anything." It had been very difficult for her to attend as many hearings and trial events as she had over the past four years, but she made herself go until resolution of the case.

She felt that it was her responsibility to be present at every court date because someone had to be there to "represent the victims."

Pomona Superior Court Judge Robert Martinez stated "The evidence is compelling that the defendant, for selfish reasons, murdered her own two children." He called her desire to start a new life with another man "narcissistic, selfish, and adolescent." He noted that Williams had many family members who would have willingly taken the boys in, and that their deaths were abhorrently unnecessary. He remarked that each of the three killings was deliberate and premeditated without question. Lastly, he remarked that he was not in the position to forgive, as "the ones in the position to forgive are not with us."

There is some question as to whether or not Williams will actually ever undergo execution. California is known for delaying executions for those on death row indefinitely. There are over 700 people who have been sentenced to death in California. However, only 13 people have put to death in California since 1976, none of whom have been the other 19 women who are already on death row in California. Neal's mother took some comfort in the resolution of the case. "The legal process will no doubt go on for probably the rest of my lifetime. But I feel like I am leaving something behind today. Something is finished," she told reporters.

One of the most notable things about Manling has been her silence. She has essentially gone radio silent since her incarceration. She has reportedly become involved with the church services within the prison where she resides, and the leader of this church testified in court that she had come to know Manling well and that she didn't feel she was "evil." It was also shared in court that many of the children who knew Devon and Ian became very traumatized upon learning of their deaths, and even more so when they learned that they were killed by their own mother.

Jan Williams maintains a blog to this day that is open to the public and started almost immediately after the death, detailing her memories, events, and coping with regard to what happened to her family. It's called Grief's Journey, and provides a raw and rare insight into the life of a survivor of a murder victim. She also keeps a fairly public Facebook page, which shows a morbid and personal look into her experience over the course of the trial. In a post from 2010, Jan writes, "In planning a suicide, it might be well to remember that it is very difficult to stab yourself repeatedly in the back, especially when your hands and fingers have been severed. That's free advice."

HUSBAND KILLER SHEENA EASTBURN

39

JAIMI WEST

Sheena Eastburn seemed to have the cards stacked against her from the start. She and Tim Eastburn were married young, when she had only just turned fifteen. The couple wed in 1990, although Tim was older, at twenty-one years of age. Talking many years later to the Joplin Globe, Alica Blevins- Sheena's mother- talked about how she should have guided her daughter's life differently, and put her on a different path.

"She was only 15 then. She was just a kid... Sheena was wild. I will admit that," she said. "For her and Tim, life was one big party. "She got herself in situations that got her into a lot of trouble. There were a lot of things that happened to her as a child that she never told me.

I just wish I could have done more for her when I had the chance. Maybe things would have turned out differently."

They were divorced a short two years later, which is often the case for couples married at such a young age.

While the divorce was described by friends as amicable, the couple maintained a sexual relationship over the years. Both were heavy drinkers, and took drugs together. In fact, whenever Sheena needed a fix, friends said, she would visit her ex-husband and provide sexual favours in return for drugs. The couple were still so close that they discussed remarriage.

Speaking about their relationship, Sheena would later say: "There were days when he loved me more than you could ever imagine and there were other days when we just fought. I was 15 years old when we got married. He was like a father and a husband to me. He was a wonderful man."

On or around November 1st, 1991, Sheena met Terry Banks for the first time, and the two immediately became close. When Banks learned of Sheena's continuing relationship with her ex-husband, however, he became "extremely possessive, jealous, and violent" according to court records. This was the catalyst for Tim's murder.

Tim Eastburn's murder

Tim was murdered using his own rifle, on November 19th 1992. He was shot in his own home in McDonald County, Missouri. The house is set a little back from the road, among the wooded hills common in McDonald County.

At the time of the murder, Sheena had only just turned seventeen, and her co-defendants were nineteen (Banks) and eighteen as well (Myers).

Two days previously, Sheena's co-defendants, Terry Banks and Matt Myers, had stolen Tim's gun- an AK-47- in a break-in along with a third man named Denashay, or 'D.J'. Johnson. They also took the chance to steal some of Tim's valuables, since stealing the gun on its own would have appeared suspicious.

The burglary took place only two weeks after Sheena had begun secretly dating her fellow co-defendant, Terry Banks. Tim and Sheena, Banks, Myers and Johnson were in fact all part of the same large circle of friends. In the time building up to the murder, the group had been drinking to excess and using drugs, a fact which probably gave the defendants the courage to do what they were about to do.

On the evening of November 19th, Sheena, Banks and Myers paid a visit to Tim at his home. It was only on that day that Sheena learned of the burglary at all; Myers and Banks had said they wanted to sell the gun- which would have fetched a good price- but Sheena convinced them not to, since it could be traced back to Tim through the serial number.

Sheena went in at first, alone, to talk with him. She asked him if he would like to come outside to take a ride on her motorbike, but he refused, saying that it was too late at night for him to want to go out.

At the time, Banks and Myers were hiding on the front porch. As Tim and Sheena continued talking, they walked through the house to the kitchen, where the pair kissed. It was only seconds later that Tim was shot with his own gun, through the window, by one of the pair outside. He quickly fell to the floor, and as he lay, Myers ran into the house to shoot him again to 'finish him off'. As he shot Tim for the second and final time, Sheena and Terry Banks ran from the house.

According to later interviews with Sheena, Tim's last words were "God forgive me for all my sins."

All three were arrested only days later, and each confessed separately to their role in Tim's murder. Each of their confessions were coherent, and none of the defendants contradicted the others with regards to their description of the day's events. However, Banks and Myers both claimed that Sheena had come up with the plot to murder Tim, a claim that she denied.

The Trial

Sheena was in prison for three years by the time she was finally put up for trial.

The facts of Tim Eastburn's murder were not challenged in court by either Terry Banks or Matt Myers. The only challenge made by Sheena was whether her actions were made after 'deliberation and cool reflection' or not- which is the metric by which murder in the first degree is judged under Missouri law. However, the defence also argued that Sheena did not necessarily understand her co-defendants' murderous intentions beforehand, a fact which also would have lessened the charge against her.

In testimony for her defence, Sheena claimed that she only learned of the burglary on the day of the murder itself. She believed that on the day that Tim died, the group of three were going to steal money and drugs from her ex-husband. She denied any knowledge of a plot to kill him. "I was supposed to go down there and get him out of the house, then we were going rob him for drugs and money."

They also planned to leave the gun at Tim's house after the robbery, rather than arouse suspicion by selling it. Sheena was quoted in interviews long after the trial, still standing by what she said. "The intent was to take back the gun that was stolen. They could track it down.

The timeline of the day's events suggested otherwise, however. Sheena's request for her ex-husband to follow her outside, and her bringing him to the kitchen with a window to the front of the house, suggested that she was trying to lead him to her death. At the very least, it was clear that it wasn't Sheena who fired the fatal shots from Tim's own gun. She claimed that Banks had shot him first in a fit of passion, after seeing the pair kiss. Myers had then delivered the final bullet.

After the shot was fired, Sheena said, "[w]e both dropped and when we dropped I crawled around to where he was, and I tried to stop the bleeding. There was nothing I could do." She was trying to paint a picture of innocence. She later talked about how she had tried to stop the bleeding with a towel and a sock that were lying nearby.

Over the course of the trial, extensive physical evidence was used in attempt to prove the group's guilt, almost sixty items in total. These included the rifle and the fragments of bullets found in Tim's body- which matched- and photo after photo of the crime scene.

D.J. Johnson also testified to the effect that the murder had been pre-meditated. He was actually a witness for the prosecution throughout the trial, as part of a plea bargain to help secure the verdicts of murder against the other three. As a result of his actions, he was given probation in connection to the charges of burglary against him, as he was part of the group that stole Tim's AK-47.

He testified that on the day of the murder itself, he overheard a three-way conversation between Myers, Banks and Sheena. In that conversation, Sheena discussed Tim with the others, claiming that he had raped her, and that she would love to see him dead. Banks, her then boyfriend, and Myers then both volunteered their services, according to Johnson. Sheena's attorneys made no attempt to discredit him, or disagree with any of his testimony.

The defence, however, argued that his testimony was unreliable due to its acquisition through a plea bargain. Johnson was offered freedom in exchange for his witness statements, and this perhaps did cast doubt on the truth of what he said. However, it was left for the jury to decide just what to make of his claims, and his statements formed a key part of the prosecution's case.

Prison Time

Whether the jury's decision would have been changed by any of this information must forever remain unknown. What they did decide, after a gruelling six hours, was that Sheena was guilty of first-degree murder.

Matt Myers was sentenced as the man who, according to the three confessions, had fired both of the fatal shots. Although he was only charged with second degree murder, among other offences related to Tim's murder (i.e. the burglary), he was sent to prison for a total of 67 years. Because of the murder being judged as of the second degree, he was eligible for parole throughout his sentence.

Terry Banks on the other hand, was sent to prison for life, on a charge of first degree murder. Sheena, too, was jailed with the same charge. The fact that Banks and Sheena were charged with first degree murder, whereas Myers (who fired one of the shots that killed Tim) wasn't, seems strange in hindsight. But Myers had made a plea bargain that saw him receive 'only' 67 years, but with the chance for parole in the future.

Indeed, Sheena's attorney filed a motion for post conviction relief in the immediate aftermath of the sentence, but this motion was denied.

"I really believed I was going to get second degree murder and I was accountable for that. I was okay with that," Sheena said in an interview, years later. She was visibly stunned when she learned of her sentence. "All I could hear was my mother in the courtroom... She was wailing," Sheena told KOAM TV. As part of the same news segment, Sheena's mother Alica Bleavins remembered the same scene: "I couldn't control it. When that's your child, and your only child, and your hands are tied..."

Terry Banks' story became more interesting in the year 2000, when he escaped from his maximum-security prison with the help of a guard. Lynnette Barnett smuggled Banks out in broad daylight, with the help of an old uniform and a fake ID. They were on the run for six weeks before they were caught. She was jailed for five years, with the help of video evidence and correspondence between her and Banks. She was, however, paroled within a year of her sentence.

Banks had another 16 years added to his sentence, although since he was already in prison for life with no option of parole, it makes little difference.

At the time of the escape, Sheena's mother said: "They put her on lock-down. They put her in the hole. They were going to leave her there until he was captured. The FBI, well, they were all over Sheena. She was the one who told them his dad was in Texas."

Signs of hope for Sheena?

There were several facts and allegations which weren't raised at trial, that in hindsight, should have been. Sheena's attorneys spoke publicly about how the outcome may have been completely different had they brought them up.

For one, IQ tests performed by Sheena in the buildup to the trial suggested that she would be incapable of organising the events as described by the prosecution.

There were also allegations that she had been raped by a McDonald County Jail when awaiting trial, and even taken to an abortion clinic. A guard who had been working there, Terrie Zornes, had been accused by Sheena of manipulating and raping her several times over the course of her time there. He had been 31, whereas she was still a minor.

Sheena claimed that he had taken her twice to the property room in 1994, and attacked her there. He was the only guard on duty at the time. According to interviews, Sheena had told her mother: "I told my mother that the officer had taken me to a property closet and had sex with me. She flipped out at that point. They locked me down in my cell.

Cut off my phone. I wasn't allowed to talk to anybody. They cut off my visitors."

Multiple reviews of the surveillance tape from the nights that Sheena alleged she had been raped gave suspicious results. While nothing of note happened, at one point in the recordings the clock would jump forward. "The hands on the clock jumped forward. A clock doesn't do that," The Sheriff of McDonald County Jail later said.

The Sherriff had nonetheless defended Zornes, claiming that the sex was "consensual". Altogether, it seemed as if both the guard and the Sheriff felt that there was something to hide.

Sheena responded with revealing comments about her past. "They kept trying to tell me it was consensual. They said: 'You know you wanted it. You know you miss it.' It was not like I fought it because there was no way I could have stopped him. I have experienced sexual abuse all of my life. I have been raped before in a violent way. After you have been in that situation, you just learn it's easier to let it go and not fight."

Moreover, in the years since the case was closed, Myers recanted on his testimony at the trial that Sheena had been the mastermind of the operation. Kent Gipson, Sheena's long time attorney, had even attained an affidavit to that effect- and that he had acquired the same from Johnson, too. This would mean that in conjunction with their defence stemming from the low IQ test score, it would be possible to argue that Sheena could not have possibly wanted Tim to be killed that day.

These facts all gave Sheena hope that she could appeal her sentence, and perhaps, win. Even if she were only able to replace her sentence with one for second degree murder, she would at least be eligible for parole in the end.

Supreme Court challenge

In interviews after her sentencing, Sheena said: "I still thought that I might get out of prison someday... I didn't realize that life without parole actually meant life without parole." She continued to maintain her innocence, saying that she had never planned a murder that day, only a robbery.

In 2012, a case went through the Alabama Supreme Court which found that the sentence of life without parole was actually unconstitutional when handed down to a minor. The case came from Alabama, but because it had been decided by the Supreme Court, cases could now be challenged nationwide. Missouri, at the time, had 84 cases of juveniles jailed for life without parole and each one of them could now seek to have their sentences reduced.

Suddenly, it seemed that Sheena might have found a way out. Once more, Sheena contacted her attorney, and they began to prepare her case for appeal. Talking to KOAM TV, her attorney Kent Gipson said "I think if you look across the spectrum of persons convicted of first degree murder, I'd say her level of culpability is among the lowest I've ever seen."

Sheena's attorney believed that she had a great chance to finally be considered for parole; and both clearly believed that she deserved the chance. "I think inevitably she will be given a parolable sentence and will be given a chance to get out of prison," Gipson said at the time. Speaking about the progress she had made while in prison, he said "She's obviously not the same person she was when she was 17 years old,I don't think any of us are... She is probably the most ideal candidate for parole any of them [prison staff] have ever seen.""

Miles Parks, a retired investigator who had worked on the case, disagreed. "Sheena Eastburn was old enough to get a driver's license, old enough to get married, old enough to know the difference between right and wrong," Parks said. "What do you think is the appropriate punishment?"

In an interview before her appeal with KOAM TV, she talked about the possibility that she might be released. "I came to that realization a long time ago, and I gave it to God, and I got peace," she had said. She still maintained that she had no role in Tim's murder, saying that "[t]here was no reason for Tim to die... None."

With her interviewer, she discussed what she missed about the outside world: "...going down to the refrigerator in the middle of the night and being able to get what you want. Walking barefoot on grass somewhere that it doesn't say 'out of bounds'. Going outside after dark. Just taking time to experience free, fresh air... I know it smells different on the other side."

Sheena wished that she could somehow find release. But she still refused to get her hopes up, stating that "You never count on anything completely until it happens because you can't let yourself get your hopes too high and then be devastated all the time. It's just a hard way to live." Over her time in prison, she had clearly lived with a hope that one day she would be set free, but had only been disappointed.

The Post-Conviction Hearing

Close friends and relatives of Tim's did not want the case re-opened. Speaking in an interview, Bobby Eastburn said, "We have been keeping track of it. We don't like what is going on. She worked hard to get in there and we don't want her out of prison. "My brother won't get a second chance. She's apparently trying to get a second chance. They say she was suffering from PTSD because of her childhood and that she was not very smart. She manipulated the situation to kill Tim. She was the mastermind behind it. She was intelligent enough to set the whole situation up."

On April 30th of 2013, three cases of minors jailed for life were put before the Missouri Supreme Court- one of them being Sheena's. Her attorney argued that the original motion that had been filed way back in 1992, for post conviction relief, should not have been denied. They argued that the judge should have then realised that such a sentence was unconstitutional.

The state argued that they did not then have the authority to challenge the constitutionality of the sentence, and so they were correct to not have allowed the defendant's motion for relief. After both sides had been presented, the court took recess so that the judges could decide on their fate.

"I am definitely guilty of second-degree murder," Sheena said in an interview around the time of her appeal.

But whether or not her appeals would be successful, she felt all along that she could never be free. "For somebody with a case like this, the prison is not really the prison. It's always going to be inside. You will always be in prison. It does not matter whether you are free or locked up, I think you will always have that inside."

But on Tuesday 25th July, that year, the Missouri Supreme Court returned the unanimous verdict that her appeal did not stand. Based on the facts of the case, they still argued that it was necessary for Sheena to be imprisoned for life.

Sheena's final hearing

It turned out that Sheena would eventually win her appeal after all.

In 2015, Sheena appealed again, under the same Supreme Court ruling as before. In her hearing of October that year, she sought the sentence of second degree murder through a plea agreement with the prosecutor. To do so, Eastburn had to waive any and all post-conviction and appeal rights- which she did.

The hearing was only 25 minutes long in total this time around. Lou Kelling, a former sheriff and supporter of Eastburn's release on parole, said at the appeal, "This is what she should have been charged with to begin with. She was an accessory to the crime. She served 10 years more time than she should have served. That on top of the fact that she was mistreated while in custody."

The defence had indeed used the same arguments as in the prior appeal, including the evidence of Sheena's IQ test, and allegations of rape and forced abortion. This time, the court decided to vacate the prior judgement. Since she had been in prison for more than 23 years, the agreement made her immediately eligible for a parole hearing.

Parole at last

Sheena Eastburn is now set to be released from prison in November, 2017. She has been judged to have served her time for second degree murder, and is getting ready for life on the outside for the first time in her life as an adult.

In a telephone interview with the Joplin Globe after it became common knowledge that she was set to be released, Eastburn said: "I now know when I will be able to move on with my life. I am grateful for a chance at parole."

In the same interview, she described how she was planning to write to the parole board and the governor in the hope that she could demonstrate just how much she had changed during her time locked away from society. "I want to show that I can be successful outside of the prison," she said. "I am very sorry for the things that happened. I have changed my life and will make better choices."

In another interview, she described her plans for the outside world. "I would go to school to become a certified personal trainer. I would love to minister to juveniles and help them know that the choices we do make have a consequence. I really do want to help people. I know that sounds crazy. But I want to help and let them know there are other choices out there no matter what your life is like because I had a bad life and childhood, but I still had choices. I did not realize that then."

And it did indeed seem that she had made genuine effort to turn her life around. In a separate interview, Sheena's mother claimed that her daughter had made every effort she possibly could from within the prison system. "Sheena has completed all of the classes that they offer at the prison. She has taken everything ... She'll sit there and the taxpayers will pay $80,000 a year to feed and house her. If she had been let out, she'd have a job and feed herself. This is something I don't understand. But we are still grateful to have a release date."

"We have waited a long time for this day to come, but we don't know when she will be released. We don't have an out day yet," Blevins said. "It could be just a matter of some paperwork. No one can really say right now."

During her time in prison, Sheena had begun full time work as an obedience trainer for rescue dogs. On top of this full time job, she had also become a qualified aerobics instructor, and found occasional work in prison helping disabled inmates. On occasion, she even led victim counselling sessions. She had spent her time as wisely as she could, and it had given her inspiration for her future release.

Before her first appeal on the unconstitutional nature of her sentence, her attorney had said "Maturity and education, things like that, should be taken into account and that's all we're really asking, that she be given the opportunity to prove to the parole board and other people that she deserves a second chance."

By the end of this year, she will be getting that chance.

HUSBAND KILLER : THE TRUE STORY OF AUDREY MARIE HILLEY

ANNA DELANEY

Audrey Marie Hilley

"That woman was pitiful," said Janice Hinds, 50, one of two neighbours who called police and cared for Hilley after spotting her sprawled on the deck of Thomason's home.

"We didn't know she was Marie Hilley. She didn't look like Marie Hilley," said Hinds, who grew up in the same Blue Mountain cotton-mill town as Hilley. "Marie Hilley was a sophisticated lady. She had pride in her looks, her dress."[1]

Her Early Life

Audrey Marie Hilley was born on June 4th, 1933 in Blue Mountain, Alabama. Her parents, Huey and Lucille Frazier, worked hard at the Linen Mill to provide for their family, and Marie (as she was known) was often looked after by relatives when her mother returned to work shortly after she was born.

Huey and Lucille loved their only child but showed their love with material things rather than affection and time. She was always well-dressed and had nice things, and as a result, Marie became rather spoilt. She was well known for her temper tantrums when things didn't go her way, and her parents, possibly out of guilt for not being there, rarely checked her for her behaviour.[2]

The Fraziers were proud people and were determined that their only child would not spend her life working in the same mills as they, and most of the town's inhabitants, had always done. They wanted more for their daughter and instilled in her an ambition to be a secretary, a lofty ambition for someone from a mill town.

In 1945, the Fraziers moved from Blue Mountain to Anniston, and Marie enrolled at Quintard Junior High School. Anniston was a whole new world to the girl who had felt she was above the rest in her old hometown. Marie went from being a big fish in a small pond to a small fish in a much more upscale lake, and for the first time in her life found herself at a disadvantage. In Anniston, all the girls wore nice dresses and what was more, some of their parents were the owners of the same mills that Marie's parents worked at.

Marie threw herself into her studies, making a name for herself as a diligent, intelligent student, and she integrated herself into new social circles – her friends were from privileged families and Marie wanted to be a part of that.

It wasn't just the teachers for whom Marie stood out, though. She was also a pretty girl and had her fair share of the attention from the boys, too. In fact, by the end of the 7th grade of Junior High School, Marie Hilley had been voted the prettiest girl in school by the yearbook staff.

It was around this time that 16-year-old Frank Hilley noticed 12-year-old Marie, and by the time he graduated High School, he was in love.[3]

Frank and Marie

In contrast to the Frazier family, who loved their daughter but showed no affection, Frank Hilley's family was warm and affectionate. The Hilleys worked in the other big industry of the area – pipe making - and even though they did not have much money, Clarence and Carrie Hilley made a happy, comfortable home for their three children – Frank, Jewel and Freeda.

Marie's parents did not approve of Frank – he was not from one of the affluent families of Anniston and Huey and Lucille wanted more for their daughter – but Marie was happy to be Frank's girl, and in return, he treated her like a princess.

Frank joined the Navy after finishing High School and was assigned to Guam but the distance between them bothered Frank. He was worried that with him so far away, and with so much time apart, Marie might find someone else so, on May 8th, 1951, before 17-year-old Marie had even finished High School, the young couple married.

Married Life

Marie remained in Anniston to finish her education and then joined Frank in Long Beach, California before the couple moved to Boston where Frank finished his stint in the Navy. It was while they were in Boston that they discovered Marie was pregnant with their first child, and the couple moved back to Anniston and bought a small home. Frank secured a job with a local foundry, and Marie found work as a secretary. Like all couples, the pair had their ups and downs, but for the most part, they seemed happy.

Their first child, Michael Hilley, was born on November 11th, 1952.

The Troubles Begin

Marie had been brought up to want the best of everything. While Frank was still in the Navy he had sent all of his paychecks home to his young wife, and yet when the time had come for her to join her new husband in California she had no money to pay for the journey. She had been spending his wages without telling him, and his parents had had to finance Marie's travel in order for her to join her new husband.

Despite the extra financial burdens having a young baby places on a family, Marie's spending didn't decrease. She wanted nice clothes and expensive home furnishings, and Frank, not liking to upset his wife, gave in to her, just as her parents had when she was a girl. Marie was a woman who was used to getting her own way.[4]

In 1959 Marie's behaviour began to become more sinister. She started taunting Frank, waving love letters she said were from other men in front of him but not letting him read them. She would then leave the torn up pieces where her husband could find them. Frank pieced them together, and it became clear that his wife had written them herself. When he confronted her she said she was afraid he didn't love her anymore and wanted to make him jealous.

By this time, Marie was spending double her take-home pay from her own job on fine clothes and luxuries. To prevent Frank, who was extremely responsible financially, from finding out she would get up early in the morning to check the mail and hide the bills.

Marie became pregnant again, and on January 14th, 1960 she gave birth to a baby daughter, whom they named Carol Marie.[5]

Carol

By the time Carol was born, things should have been looking up for the family. Frank had been promoted at work, and Marie had developed a reputation as a first class executive secretary. However, as the family's income rose, so did Marie's spending. Furthermore, she was becoming known for a peculiar situation at work. While her bosses loved her for her politeness and diligence, her co-workers greatly disliked her. They found her to be very judgemental of those around her and felt that she put on airs and graces and acted as if her co-workers were 'beneath' her. When she became disliked she would leave, and complain to friends and family that her colleagues had 'ganged up' on her and driven her from her job. Her employers, though, always gave her exemplary references, and she never found it difficult to get another job. In fact, Marie Hilley worked for some of the most powerful and affluent men in Anniston.[6]

Marie was disappointed with her daughter, Carol. She wanted her daughter to wear pretty dresses and have bows in her hair, while Carol was more of a tomboy and would often go to football games with her father. The pair developed a close father/daughter relationship and Marie was deeply resentful and jealous. She lamented the fact that her daughter was not feminine and demure and the pair argued constantly. Marie was much closer to her son, Mike, and like her parents before her never dished out discipline. Materially, the children wanted for nothing. Emotionally, it was a different story.

Going Up in the World

In 1962, Marie instigated a move to McClellan Boulevard, which was much closer to the houses of the affluent residents of Anniston that she so desperately tried to emulate. She felt that they were 'her' people. That same year, Marie's parents – Huey and Lucille moved in with the Hilleys.[7]

Marie's behaviour was becoming more and more out of control, and Frank was becoming increasingly concerned. He would often sit up with her during the night as she shook violently, unable to calm her. Perhaps the financial hole she had dug for the family was beginning to take its toll on Marie's psyche – by this time she had opened a Post Office Box and was having some of her bills sent there in order to avoid detection by Frank.

When the money ran out Marie started taking out loans. Frank was a well-respected man in the area and loans were secured against his good name and standing in the community. But creditors became concerned when bills and loan payment dates came and went without being settled, as Frank had always been a man who paid on time.[8]

On December 11th, 1965, Marie's father, Huey, died of cancer at the age of 57.[9]

In 1972, Mike graduated from High School and decided to pursue a career in the ministry, for which he went away to college.

Marie's behaviour towards her daughter, Carol, became more extreme. She often accused her of being a lesbian and would rant at Carol's female friends. Her paranoia at being found out in the lies regarding money must have been affecting her, because she also, around this time, stopped Frank from talking to his friends on the 'phone. It was also around this period of time that Frank Hilley became sick.[10]

Frank

During 1974 Frank had long periods of sickness. He put his frequent illnesses down to something he'd eaten, but soon the fatigue, vomiting and nausea could not be explained away by food. One day Frank came home from work early after succumbing to yet another bout of sickness, to find his wife in bed with her boss. His wife's spending suddenly made sense – she was sleeping with her employers for money. Frank was disgusted with his wife's behaviour but felt too ill and weak to deal with it. Instead, he turned to his son, Mike, who was by this time an ordained minister.[11]

However, that phone call, in which Frank arranged to meet Mike in Georgia where he now lived, was overheard by Audrey, who was listening in on an extension. From that moment on, Frank's symptoms worsened considerably, and he became seriously ill.[12]

On May 19th, 1975 Frank couldn't stand it any longer, and he consulted Dr Earl Jones, who diagnosed him initially with a viral stomach ache.[13] Dr Earl prescribed various medications, but nothing seemed to be helping. Frank's sister Freeda came to visit him, and he told her that he feared he was going to die, as he had never been so sick. He also told her that Marie had been administering him medicine via a syringe on the Dr's orders.[14]

On May 23rd, 1975, Frank was admitted to the Regional Medical Center. Tests indicated liver failure, and subsequently infectious hepatitis.[15] Frank was desperately ill, jaundiced and hallucinating. Mike, who had travelled to be with his father, had to restrain Frank from jumping out of the window. In the early hours of May 25th, Mike left the hospital to pick up his Grandmothers so that they could see Frank, but when he returned his mother was asleep and his father was dead. Frank Hilley was 45.[16]

Because of Frank's sudden death, an autopsy was performed, with Marie's blessing. Tests showed that Frank did indeed have hepatitis, along with swelling of the lungs and kidneys, inflammation of the stomach, and bilateral pneumonia.[17]

Life After Frank

With Frank's death being confirmed as being of natural causes, Marie made a claim on his life insurance and received a payment of $31,140.[18] Marie went on a spending spree, indulging her love of luxury items. She bought new clothes, jewelery, and a new car. Her mother, Lucille, was still living with Marie and Carol and received a diamond ring. Carol herself was treated to numerous gifts, including a car and a stereo. It was hardly the behaviour of a grieving widow.[19]

In 1976 Mike and his then wife Teri moved in with the family. Shortly after Frank's death, Lucille had been diagnosed with cancer. Her health was failing and they were happy to help. However, it wasn't a good move for the young couple. Marie was restless, and often complained to anyone who would listen that nobody loved her, and would frequently complain about her boss and her job. She was highly dissatisfied with her life, and to make matters worse Marie and Carol fought endlessly, making family life fraught. Mike would often find himself torn between his mother, who would constantly demand his attention, and his wife, Teri, who had begun experiencing ill health since moving in with Marie. Hospitalised four times with illness, Teri also suffered a miscarriage, and the young couple decided to move out.

They found an apartment and were ready to move in, but the night before their move Marie's house caught fire. Mike and Teri moved into their apartment, with Marie, Carol and Lucille in tow. Repairs were soon made to Marie's house, but the night before his mother was due to go home, Mike's neighbour's apartment suffered the same fate and went up in flames. Mike and Teri had no choice but to move back in with Marie, Carol and Lucille. They were back where they began.[20]

A Strange Series of Events

Mike and Teri finally found their own home and moved away from Marie. On January 4th, 1977, Lucille lost her battle against widespread, aggressive cancer. Marie again came into money – a small sum of $600 from a burial policy.

Marie became well known to the local police. She was constantly reporting strange occurrences at her home. As well as petty thefts, she claimed that a fire had been started in her closet late one night. Coincidentally, Marie's neighbour, Doris Ford reported an almost identical fire in her own house (to which Marie had a key) the same night. There followed a succession of reports by both women of nuisance phone calls and other grievances.

Marie came up with many theories about where the harassment of both herself and her neighbour was coming from. She told Detective Gary Caroll that she suspected someone at the phone company of making the calls, as the calls seemed only to happen when the trace was taken off of her phone. She also claimed that one of her former employers had tried to force her to have sex and was harassing her because of her refusal. Yet another theory put forward by Marie was that, shortly after Frank's death, two men had arrived at her house demanding repayment of gambling debts.

When police put a trace on Doris Ford's phone, however, the calls were traced back to the Jenkins Manufacturing Plant, which just so happened to be where Marie was working.[21]

In 1978, Marie and Carol moved to Florida to live with Mike and Teri. Carol had just graduated, and Marie found herself a job in an office. Her out of control spending habits continued to cause problems when she ran up over $600 on Mike's credit card, promising to pay him back. This living arrangement only lasted a few short months, however, before Marie and Carol returned to Anniston.[22]

Mike and Teri were happy to see Marie leave. By that time they had a baby son called Joshua, and Mike feared that Marie would take the baby and disappear as she seemed to have an unhealthy fixation on him.[23]

Carol's Turn

Marie had no home of her own to return to when she and Carol moved back to Anniston. At first, they stayed with Freeda, Frank's sister, and then they moved in with Carrie Hilley, Frank's mother. Once they were settled at Carrie's house, the strange happenings recommenced. Items went missing, phone lines were cut, and small fires were started. Illness also struck the household – Carrie Hilley started suffering from nausea and vomiting.

Marie started a new job, and very quickly started an affair with her boss, Harold Dillard, and began manipulating him to leave his wife. At the same time, she also started seeing Calvin Robertson, an old school friend. Calvin believed Marie when she told him she had cancer and needed expensive treatment, and he gladly gave her the money for the 'fictitious' illness. When Marie told him some time later that she was now cancer-free he was elated, and so smitten that he would have done anything for her.

It was also during this time that Marie began buying insurance policies. Not only did she take out fire insurance, cancer insurance, and her own life insurance, she also took out insurance policies on the lives of her two children. Mike was insured for $25,000 while Carol had two policies on her life, totalling $39,000.

Carol's senior prom came in April 1979. During the evening Carol started to feel ill. It wasn't enough to make her leave the party, though, so she ignored her symptoms. The next day, however, she was so ill during a church service that she had to leave the service early and vomited in the car park. Coincidentally, Carrie Hilley had also taken ill at church and was taken to hospital after fainting.[24]

By August 1979 Carol had been admitted to the Emergency Room several times with nausea and vomiting. After yet another episode of sickness in August, Marie gave her daughter an injection into her hip, which she said would ease the nausea. Instead of easing, however, Carol's illness took a serious downturn. Not only did the injection not ease Carol's sickness, it also caused her fingers and legs to become numb and weak.

On August 22nd, 1979 she was admitted to the Anniston Hospital by Dr Warren Sarrell. When, by August 29th Dr Sarrell had been unable to find a cause for Carol's symptoms, he sent her for a psychiatric evaluation at the Carraway Methodist Hospital in Birmingham. While under the care of Dr John Elmore, Carol was given two further injections by her mother – injections which, she was told, would help with her weak legs. She told Carol that the injections had been supplied by Doris Ford, who was a registered nurse, and that Carol could tell no-one as Doris would get into trouble if she was found out.

On September 18th, 1979, with Carol still in the hospital, Marie asked Dr Elmore what was wrong with her daughter. He told her that she was suffering from vitamin deficiencies and malnutrition, and, in his opinion, lead poisoning. Carol took exception to this diagnosis and, against Dr Elmore's advice, discharged Carol from the hospital.

On September 19th, Carol was once again admitted to the hospital, this time to the University of Alabama Hospital in Birmingham. The same day, Marie was arrested as her fraudulent ways finally caught up with her. Her arrest was what, ultimately, saved Carol's life. Marie was taken in for questioning, and Carol was examined by Dr Brian Thompson, who noticed that, along with the numbness in her hands and feet, Carol also had striations on her nails, called Aldridge Mee's Lines. He explained that these markings were typical of arsenic poisoning, and ordered tests on Carol's hair.

The initial findings revealed that Carol had over 50 times the normal arsenic level of human hair. Shockingly, when more detailed tests were carried out on October 3rd, 1979 they showed that the hair close to Carol's scalp had over 100 times the normal levels, while hair further down the hair shaft the levels were lower, right down to zero at the ends. This indicated, according to Forensic Scientist John Case, that Carol had been systematically poisoned with arsenic over a period of four to eight months, with the dosages given in increasingly higher strengths.

Furthermore, with Marie unable to be with her daughter, Carol's conditioned improved dramatically during her time at the hospital.[25]

On the strength of these findings, Frank Hilley's body was exhumed, and once again large levels of arsenic were found. His cause of death was changed to that of arsenic poisoning. The same substance was also discovered to have been present in both Lucille Frazier and Carrie Hilley (who had died recently) at the time of their deaths, although not fatal amounts.[26]

On October 9th, 1979, while still incarcerated for the fraudulent charges, Marie Hilley was arrested for the attempted murder of Carol. As part of their ongoing, and increasingly serious, investigations the Anniston police found a vial in Marie's purse – a vial which testing confirmed contained arsenic.

On November 9th, 1979, Marie made bail and was released, under the name of Emily Stephens, to a local motel. However, Marie was not going to just sit and await her trial, and somewhere between October 9th and October 18th, Marie disappeared. A note was found in her motel room, suggesting that she 'might' have been kidnapped.

Audrey Marie Hilley was now a fugitive and would remain so for more than three years.[27]

A New Identity

There were only a few clues for the police to go on after Marie disappeared. Margaret Key, Marie's Aunt, reported that her home had been broken into and that her car and some clothes had disappeared. The police called in the FBI, but once the car was found abandoned in Georgia the trail went cold very quickly.

On January 11th, 1980, Marie Hilley, still a fugitive, was indicted for the murder of her husband, Frank Hilley.

Marie, meanwhile, had assumed a new identity in Florida. Robbi Hannon, as she was now known, was working her charm on a man called John Homan. Robbi told John tales of her imaginary tragic past, and John, who hadn't had the easiest of lives himself, fell for both the stories and for Robbi. She told him that she had lost her children in a car accident and John felt as though he had found a kindred spirit.

He fell in love, hook, line, and sinker.

On May 29th, 1981 Robbi and John were married, after which they moved to Marlow, New Hampshire. They both found work there and rented a house. Robbi's new job was in customer service at the Central Screw Corporation, where she excelled. The men found her to be fun, while her co-workers, for the most part, found her pleasant, although a few took a dislike to her. She regaled the staff with stories of a wealthy family in Texas, whose fortune she would inherit one day, and garnered sympathy by telling them about her two children dying in a car accident.

She would also talk of an identical twin sister called Teri Martin, who lived in Texas, making frequent reference to her.

Robbi would, from time to time, complain of searing headaches, and told John that she was seeking treatment from specialists. Until one day, Robbi came to John and told him it had been discovered that she was suffering from an incurable blood disease. It was her twin sister, Teri, who would be looking after Robbi when she made one last trip to Texas in search of a cure, and in September 1982, Robbi left Marlow to seek treatment.

Of course, there was no incurable disease, and no twin sister, either. Robbi only stayed in Texas for a few days, and then made her way to Florida, where she bleached her hair blond, and found work as a secretary, using the name Teri Martin. During her six weeks at her new job, Teri confided in her boss, Jack McKenzie, about her terminally ill twin sister Robbie. In early November, Teri called Jack and told him Robbi had died, and that she was needed in New Hampshire.

On November 10th, 'Teri' called John Homan and told him his wife had died, and the following day she flew back to New Hampshire.

During her time away, 'Teri' had lost a lot of weight, and changed her hair color to blond, so John easily accepted that this was his dead wife's twin sister. The pair went to the local paper and placed an obituary for Robbi, and then John took Teri to his wife's workplace – The Central Screw Corporation – and introduced the workers to Robbi's twin sister. While some of the staff accepted Teri's appearance, some did not and were highly suspicious.

Teri insisted on moving in with John Homan, saying they needed to help each other grieve, and she found herself a job as a secretary at a book printing company.

Meanwhile, the suspicions were still rising at Robbi's old workplace, and a few of the doubters decided to take a closer look into Robbi's obituary. Their suspicions were confirmed when they discovered that the details mentioned in the paper were fictitious, and they took those suspicions to the police.

Arrested

On January 12th, 1983, the police apprehended Teri at work. They had been watching her and thought she might be another fugitive, Terry Lynn Clifton. However, when they asked her her name she told them it was Audrey Marie Hilley, and that she was wanted for fraud. The local police ran a check on her name and discovered that she was wanted for much more than bad checks.

On January 19th, 1983, Marie was brought back to Anniston. Carol was desperate to see her mother, to find some answers, but although Marie professed her love for her daughter she gave no explanation for the poisoning. Prosecutors were worried that Carol's love for her mother would go in Marie's favour and that Carol would not say anything against her mother.

They needn't have worried.

Carol's testimony about her mother giving her the injections was solid. Marie had told her attorneys that after her arrest in 1979 she had been interviewed but she failed to mention that that interview had been recorded. During that interview, Marie admitted to giving Carol the injections and the recording was there for all to hear. Carol's defense fell apart.

The jury needed only three hours to return their verdicts – guilty of the murder of Frank Hilley, and of the attempted murder of Carol Hilley.

Judge Sam Monk sentenced Marie to life imprisonment for Frank's murder, plus twenty years for the poisonings, and on June 9th, 1983, Marie was taken to Tutwiler State Women's Prison in Wetumpka, Alabama.

Marie's Escape

Marie was a perfect prisoner. She never caused trouble and was classified as a minimum security prisoner. This classification meant that she was eligible for leave from the prison. Between late 1986 and February 1987, Marie had left prison for eight hours on four occasions, returning on time with each leave.

On February 19th, 1987, Marie left the prison on a three-day leave pass. John had, by this time, moved to Anniston so that he and his wife could spend her leave together whenever they could.

On February 22nd, Marie arranged to meet John at her parents' graves. Marie never showed up, and John found, instead, a note from his wife.

"I hope you will be able to forgive me," it read. *"I'm getting ready to leave. It will be best for everybody. We'll be together again. Please give me an hour to get out of town."*

John took the note to the police, and, given Marie's past cunning, they assumed she was already far out of state, and started, once again, searching for her.[28]

Her Death

Marie hadn't gone far. On February 26th, 1987, Aniston police received a phone call. Marie had been found huddled behind a house, apparently having wandered in the woods for four days. The weather had been terrible – heavy rain and low temperatures – and Marie was suffering from hypothermia and delirium. Marie started having convulsions, and, in the ambulance on the way to the hospital, Audrey Marie Hilley took her last breath.

On February 28th, 1987, Marie was buried next to her husband, Frank, at their children's request.[29] Her second husband, John Homan, died two years later in 1989 while working as a caretaker in Anniston. He intervened in a fight and was stabbed to death. Marie's note to John, in which she said that they would be together again, had come true a lot sooner than anyone would have predicted.[30]

HOUSEWIFE, MOTHER & KILLER : THE TRUE STORY OF KIM HRICKO

DARLA PUGH

PROLOGUE

Kim Hricko was getting ready to kill her husband the night they attended a Valentine's Murder Mystery Party. Kim was a woman who was intelligent and determined, the irony of the play's theme was not lost on her.

It was destiny calling.

She watched with rapt attention as the actors went through the motions. A wedding bride took out a blue vial and poured the "poisonous" contents into her groom's champagne glass.

She has the right idea, Kim thought.

Looking over at her husband Steve, she imagined him in the place of the actor on stage, choking to death.

Could it be that easy?

CHAPTER ONE

"Kim Hricko was one of those people that you look at and say 'I would never have guessed,'" forensic psychologist Paula Orange said. "Something inside her snapped when she wanted out of her marriage. It could have been so simple. Call a lawyer and file for divorce. Kim wanted a lot more than that. She wanted blood."

Steve and Kim Hricko would be introduced by their mutual friends Maureen and Mike Miller at Penn State in 1984. Their temperaments seemed to be the perfect complement to one another, they would have a yin-yang compatibility.

"Kim was a very gregarious personality," Maureen said. "She was very outgoing. Very friendly. Everybody liked her."

"Steve was my best friend since seventh grade," Mike said. "Corny as it sounds we were kinda each others brother that we didn't have. My wife had set up a double date. He (Steve) was smitten by her. Thought she was very attractive. Basically, they hit it off and from that point on started dating."

Steve was a burly figure at 6'3" and 245 lbs. He was a star college football player but was on the shy side.

"He was a big teddy bear," Maureen said. "He just wanted everybody that he loved to be happy and for him to take care of them."

Neither Kim or Steve dated much before their union. Kim had a distant relationship with her father after her own parents divorced. Her mother would remarry a man that would sexually and physically abuse her.

Steve and Kim would marry and have a daughter. Nine years into their marriage, Steve would still be smitten by the woman that the Millers had set him up with. Kim, however, would have feelings of resentment that built up over time.

Temperamentally, the couple did not match up well. Steve was an introvert. Kim an extrovert. Kim hung out with doctors and nurses while Steve just wanted to stay home. He didn't feel welcome into Kim's elite social circle, put off by their large houses and flashy cars.

But Steve remained in love with Kim despite that over the years she did not treat him with the same warmth as she once did. She was now cold and disinterested toward her spouse.

Steve blamed himself for the deterioration and began working to save his marriage.

His efforts would only serve to pour fuel on the fire...

CHAPTER TWO

Kim fed up with the loveless relationship, suggested that they get a divorce but Steve refused. He also dismissed the idea of counseling but after nine years he finally saw it as a last resort.

Steve went to counseling on his own and began taking steps to show Kim how much he truly cared. One of the first things he did was write his wife a long, heartfelt love letter.

Kim shared the letter with some of her friends who remarked at how beautiful it was. But Steve's words of love and devotion had no effect on Kim.

"Can you believe this shit?" Kim mocked as she read some passages aloud. "I am willing to do whatever it takes to save our marriage. It takes two of us. But I know we can do it. Together."

"I think that's sweet," her friend remarked.

"Gag me," Kim rolled her eyes. "Trust me, when you've been married as long as I have this kind of syrupy shit only makes you sick."

"I wish my husband would write me love letters."

"No," Kim said. "You don't. They keep coming and they don't stop. He's smothering me and following me around the house like a puppy dog."

Steve's renewed efforts to rekindle a long dead marriage were now being met with resentment. He was earnest in displaying his affection and becoming more communicative with Kim.

"Let's talk about our feelings," he said to his wife who stiffened with his every touch.

Kim would go to work eager to vent. She would open up about her marital difficulties to anyone who was willing to listen. She found a confidante in Jennifer Gowen.

"He is suffocating me," Kim told Gowen. "Stifling me. Following me around the damn house the whole time and cuddling with me at night. I can't even breathe. He's always asking me where I'm going or what I'm doing. Now he's calling me on my cell just to say 'Hi'. He never used to do that. It is annoying as shit."

But Steve was merely following the advise of his counsel. He had not dated much before Kim and she was his first serious relationship. He had no idea what to do when the relationship turned sour.

"It has to be said that Steve was on the receiving end of some very bad counseling advice," Orange said. "Appeasement never works and that is something that any decent psychiatrist or counselor should know. He kept turning the other cheek with Kim and that just fueled her resentment of him even more. This isn't to justify his murder, of course."

With his counseling session inspired efforts not yielding any results, Steve became distraught. He had done everything by the book but it wasn't working. He called his close friend Mike and opened up about his marriage and job difficulties.

"I don't know what to do, man," Steve said, his voice quaking with emotion. "I don't want to lose her. She's my life. My family is my everything. I feel like I've already lost her."

"Take it easy," Mike said. "We'll figure something out."

"What do you think I should do?" Steve asked.

"You need to take her out," Mike said "Someplace special. You know. Make a memory."

"Yeah," Steve said. "I know that. But I'm at a loss at how to go about it. I've tried everything."

"Tell you what," Mike said. "You come over to the Golf Resort."

"Harbourtowne?"

"I'll make sure you get the honeymoon cottage we have here. The very best one."

"You're too cool, Mike."

"Anytime, brother."

Mike worked at the Harbourtowne Golf Resort and set up the accommodations for his good friend and his wife. The place was hosting a Valentine's Day Murder Mystery play. Mike knew that the place worked wonders for romance. If there was anyplace that could rekindle the spark in a relationship, the resort would be it.

But Steve didn't know that Kim already had a romance of her own. His name was Brad Winkler.

CHAPTER THREE

Kim had met Brad Winkler when she was planning out the bachelorette party for her co-worker, Jennifer Gowen. Jennifer had brought Brad to the wedding shower ahead of time and the United States Marine was the only man at the party aside from Steve.

Kim and the young man hit it off immediately. She gave him a ride home along with Norma Walz after the party was over. They dropped off Brad at his aunt's house and Kim watched from the car as the young man made his way inside.

"He was in a bad marriage," Kim said to Norma. "Pretty sad. He's a nice guy. Jesus. The girl who catches him is going to be a lucky one. He's really sweet."

Kim returned home and was chastised by Steve for spending so much time with Brad. He had no idea of the affair to come.

Jennifer Gowen would get married and enlist the aid of Brad to help around the house while she was away on her honeymoon. Jennifer had a one-year-old daughter and Brad would babysit the girl and do some chores around the place.

Kim would come over and help out with the baby on the day Gowen left.

The affair with Brad would begin that night. They would have their trysts at Jen's townhouse while his cousin was still on her honeymoon. When Jennifer returned, the couple would continue their affair at the home of Brad's aunt.

Kim was equally open about her affair with Brad Winkler among friends as she was about her dissatisfaction with her marriage.

"I'm seeing someone," Kim said to Rachel, her college friend.

"You're having an affair?"

"Its just sex," Kim said, shrugging her shoulder. "I'm not going to marry this guy."

Kim kept up the charade on the home front as she plotted her next move. The change in her behavior made Steve believe that his efforts were working as he chronicled in his journal.

"Life at home is improving," Steve wrote. "I am looking forward to Valentine's weekend at Harbourtowne with Kim. She called twice today and said 'I love you' without me saying it first. I was very happy. Kim and I have not made love yet and I want to but I will wait as long as it takes. I love her...I believe I know what being in love really is. We have been married nine years but I feel like we just started dating."

Sadly, four days after Steve wrote those words in his journal Kim was off buying Brad Winkler a Valentine's Day gift.

"Brad, I really want to give you all these gifts in person but I guess the Pentagon had a different idea," Kim wrote. "I am so proud of what you do so I'll just go on missing you. Have a nice weekend at home, baby. I look forward to seeing you soon. Happy Valentine's Day, sir. I love you so very much. Hugs and Kisses, Kim."

While Steve had an optimistic view of their future life together, Kim continued to tell anyone with a listening ear about her dissatisfaction.

"There is a lot of verbal abuse," Kim said to Theresa Armstrong, one of her neighbors. "From both of us. He doesn't do anything. I do everything. I am unhappy and don't want to be married to him anymore."

She then went to her job at Holy Cross Hospital and told her co-worker Norma Walz about her problems.

"I've been in a bad marriage for a long time," Kim said. "Me and Steve have been having problems for a long time. A very long time."

"I always suspected that something wasn't right," Norma said.

"I've been living a lie," Kim nodded. I wanted him to go to counseling two years ago. Now he's going. And he's driving me crazy."

Steve's constant fawning and pandering annoyed Kim so much that she began thinking about what life would be like without him.

"You know if my husband dies we'd be better off than if we got a divorce," Kim told one of her neighbors. "Steve doesn't make that much money. He's a groundskeeper. We get a divorce and I'm paying him alimony. But if he died, well, if he died we would inherit $450,000 from his life insurance."

"That's a morbid thing to think about," the neighbor said, trying to laugh it off.

"You read about these stories all the time. The husband killing off the wife and vice-versa. I always wondered why they did it instead of just getting a divorce. It's the life insurance. Just like in the movies."

"What was lost in Kim's rationalizing was the fact that the killers most always get caught," Orange said. "But in her mind, she was the special one. Narcissists always think like that. Like they are the special one that won't get caught. Still, Kim needed that reassurance from her peers that she was doing the right thing as crazy as it sounds."

After not getting a receptive response from her neighbor, Kim once again turned to Jennifer Gowen.

"Steve would be better off dead," Kim said, using the same line on Jennifer. "We talked about getting a divorce but Steve doesn't want that. Even if he did he is going to try and turn Anna against me or try to keep her. He doesn't have a life outside our marriage so he is better off dead anyway."

"You really shouldn't talk like that. Let alone think like that."

"Why not? I thought about telling him about Brad but I think he would just get depressed or suicidal. Then I would not be able to collect the insurance if he killed himself."

"You think he'd kill himself?"

"Probably," Kim said. "So I have to figure something else out. You know there was this serial killer. I forgot her name. But she would go around in the children's ward and shoot the kids up with Succinylcholine. It is a muscle paralyzer. No way to trace it."

Kim would later inform Gowen that if she could kill Steve and get away with it that she "would do it tomorrow."

Seeking other alternatives aside from poisoning, Kim approached fellow surgical tech Ken Burges in the locker room of the hospital.

"Hi, Ken."

"Hey there," Ken said.

"Do you know of anyone that could kill my husband?"

"What?" Ken asked. He thought Kim was playing a joke.

"Do you know anyone that can, you know, kill someone? For a price."

"I'm insulted that you would ask me that. Do I look that sketchy to you?"

Burges had been convicted of welfare fraud in Virginia a couple of years before obtaining his job at the hospital. Because of this, Kim may have presumed that he would be the type of person who would know people capable of such an act.

"I got $50,000 for anyone who could do something like that."

"You got the wrong dude," Ken said. "The wrong guy."

"Forget I even asked," Kim said.

"You work in the operating room," Ken advised. "You could just put him to sleep."

Ken didn't know that Kim already had that idea in mind.

Kim began to plot out details of the murder. She needed to do something that was untraceable. This called for poison. She had to burn away any evidence so her attack had to take place away from home.

She ran her plan by a college friend of hers, Rachel McCoy. Kim justified her actions by demonizing her husband. She talked about his unwillingness to do stuff with her as he was a homebody and kept a messy home. Their personalities were too different.

Then without warning, she began articulating her plan to kill Steve with the poison and then setting the place on fire.

It was almost as if she wanted Rachel to poke any holes in her plan should she miss anything.

Rachel tried to talk Kim out of the hare-brained idea to no avail. She suggested simply getting a divorce but Kim was convinced that killing Steve was "easier." Rachel also brought up the fact that she was robbing their daughter, Anna, of a father.

"She would be better off without him," Kim said.

Whatever Rachel suggested, Kim had an answer for.

Her mind was made up.

Steve had to go.

CHAPTER FOUR

Kim knew that the drug she had to obtain was Succinylcholine. It would be readily available to her as she did her rounds through the hospital. Just walk by a tray of meds in the surgery unit and lift one of the vials. Easy peasy.

"I'm going to get this drug," Kim told her friend Rachel. "It will paralyze Steve. Stop his breathing and then I'll set the curtains on fire with a candle or a cigar. He won't be able to move and then he'll die of smoke inhalation. Nobody will know shit."

Kim would not take into account the fact that her husband was a healthy and robust man with no medical history. That would certainly draw suspicion.

"This would be the only logical explanation for what brought about Steven Hricko's death," prosecuting attorney Robert Dean said.

"Because there was nothing else wrong with him. His body organs were in fine shape, there was no trauma. It had to have been this. She had to have carried through her plan."

"Kim was determined," Orange said. "She wanted her cake and eat it too. It is a head scratcher as to why she didn't pursue a divorce but the mind of a sociopath works differently. She wanted a clean break. If she had gotten a divorce, then Steve would have remained in her life forever the next ten years because of their daughter. She wanted to erase him from the picture and nothing and nobody was going to talk her out of it."

The planned romantic getaway loomed on the horizon for Valentine's Day weekend. Steve looked forward to their alone time together with giddy excitement. He told his counselor that this would be the turning point where the sparks of romance would once again be rekindled.

But Kim looked toward the weekend with dread. She had told Jennifer Gowen that she had only had sex with Steve once in the past six months and the experience left her feeling repulsed.

"I'm not looking forward to the trip," Kim said in her own counseling session.

"Why?" her counselor asked. "It may be an opportunity to rekindle some passion."

"I'm tired and really don't feel up to the trip. It's a long drive. It is going to be miserable."

Then a light bulb flashed in Kim's mind. The resort would be the perfect place.

The perfect place to put her plans into effect.

CHAPTER SIX

Valentine's Day weekend arrived.

Steve had romance on his mind. His forehead perspired as he felt the anxiety of trying to save his marriage.

Kim had Brad Winkler on her mind as she looked out the car window.

Then her mind drifted to murder.

She had to set everything up just right. Inject Steve. Burn the cottage room. Then tell the police her story and stick with it no matter what.

Kim and Steve drove from their home in Laurel, Maryland to St Michaels. It would be a 75-mile to a romantic getaway that many had christened as the "Heart & Soul of Chesapeake Bay."

But the couple arrived at their cottage and found the place to be freezing. Kim started a fire in the wood stove then made some coffee.

The conversation was muted and awkward. They decided to watch some TV before looking out the window and taking in the view of the bay. It was windy and the the cold, damp weather chased them back inside

Preparing for the dinner, Steve popped a few Effexor tablets for his depression which had gotten worse in recent weeks. He also took an anti-anxiety medication called Xanax and a muscle relaxant called Flexeril.

Getting dressed, they attended the interactive murder mystery dinner called THE BRIDE WHO CRIED. The actors staged a re-enactment of a woman killing her soon to be husband. The actors encouraged audience members to ask the actors questions in an attempt to find out who the murderer was.

Kim enjoyed the play immensely. When the actors called for audience participation, she was one of two women who went out onto the stage and began asking questions like a detective.

The play now over, Kim and Steve returned to their cottage. Not yet having their fill of entertainment, the couple would watch the comedy film "Tommy Boy". They got a good laugh out of it but according to Kim they "still did not talk about our problems."

Steve then fell asleep.

Kim stood over him like a predator then went to the bathroom to prepare her lethal cocktail of succinylcholine. Building up her nerve, she finally did the move that she had been practicing in her head for two years.

Kim pulled aside the bed sheet and injected the syringe into his neck.

I'll burn the body. That will get rid of the puncture wound.

Kim also knew that the drug she administered only caused paralysis. It didn't affect a patient's level of consciousness.

So when Kim set the room on fire, Steve would know that he was being burned to death.

And he wouldn't be able to do anything about it.

The thought made Kim smile. She didn't want to just kill him. She wanted to make him suffer. To humiliate him.

Kim pulled the now paralyzed but awake Steve off the bed and dropped him to the floor. She doused his body with lighter fluid.

Kim, what are you doing? Steve looked up at his wife, unable to move or speak.

"Call it the perfect crime," she whispered in his ear as if reading his thoughts.

He stared straight up at the ceiling, catching Kim's movements in the corner of his eye.

He heard a matchstick strike against a box.

Then he felt a sharp pain race up his body as she set him ablaze.

I can't move, Steven thought as terror and pain engulfed him.

I can't breathe.

I can't breathe.

Kim, what are you doing?

I brought you here to save our marriage. I have done what I could do making this better.

I love you. Please don't do this!

Kim poured more of the lighter fluid onto Steve's body. She lit another match and threw it on him.

"She injected him with succinylcholine and watched him suffocate," Maureen said. "And lit him on fire. How much colder could it get."

CHAPTER FIVE

Kim Hricko walked into the resort reception area with a calm demeanor. She had her ear to her cell phone which was turned upside down.

"I need to talk to someone who works here," she informed desk clerk Elaine Phillips.

"I work here," Elaine said, expecting Kim's response being anything from wanting more towels to complaining about faulty air conditioning.

"My room is on fire."

"Is there anyone else in the room?" Phillips asked.

"Yeah," she said without emotion. "My husband."

"What room are you in?" Elaine asked, making her way around the corner of the desk.

Elaine and another hotel employee hurried into the courtyard of the resort.

"You smell that?" Elaine asked. "Something is definitely burning."

The two sprinted to cottage number 506 at the end of the resort. The door was shut but there was a tiny opening in the sliding door in the rear.

Smoke filled the room. They could barely see one foot in front of them. Kneeling down, one of the employees saw the the prone figure of a man inside. He crawled in, braving the smoke and pulled the body to safety on the back porch.

It was too late.

Steve Hricko, burned to a crisp.

The man had died with a Playboy magazine at his side with his pajama pants down at his knees as if he collapsed while masturbating.

"I want to see his dead body," Kim said as she milled around with the hotel guests watching the scene.

"I thought it was odd," one of the guests said. "Because no one had pronounced anyone to be dead yet."

Kim gave her statement to the Sheriff then called their best friends, Mike and Maureen Miller.

"It's the last thing you expect when you receive a phone call at night," Maureen said. "When the phone rings at night you know that it's not anything good."

"My wife answered the phone," Mike Miller said. "And sort of roused me a little bit and said that there's was an incident in Steve and Kim's room. Kim's requesting that you come down there as soon as possible.

The Millers were shocked at the sudden death of Steve. They were even more shocked at the demeanor of Kim when they went to console her.

"I didn't expect her to be anything less than a hysterical woman whose husband passed away," Maureen said. "She was the exact opposite. Just exact opposite."

Kim told everyone that Steve was drunk and made advances toward her. He groped and fondled her but she didn't want to have sex. They argued and she left the cottage.

Mike knew that something was fishy. His friend Steve was not a drinker.

Did Kim plan this out?

"They said the fire started because of him carelessly smoking," Mike said. "Steve doesn't smoke. All the years I've known Steve, I've never seen him smoke a cigarette, a cigar. He despised being around people that smoked."

An autopsy was performed and forensic pathologist Janis Amatuzio, like Mike Miller, quickly realized that something was amiss.

"Steven's body was found in a fire," Amatuzio said. "The major question for the forensic pathologist is that did he die of the fire or not. When there was no soot in the airways, when there was no damage to the lungs. It suggested that Steven was dead before the fire started."

"Steven was not drunk that night," prosecuting attorney Robert Dean said. "The drug tests and the autopsy shows that. Steve was not drunk."

The picture didn't fit. Steve was not a drinker nor was he a smoker. But friends and family could not believe the worst about Kim Hricko. The fun and outgoing mother could not have killed her own husband, the man who adored her for the past nine years.

Could she?

"Was she really capable of doing this?" Maureen asked. "Everybody was saying it but again, I ignored it and just pushed it back and said that she wasn't capable of doing it. Man, was I wrong."

CHAPTER SIX

Police began their investigation and discovered that Kim left a trail of incriminating conversations as well as evidence.

"Kim was too smart for her own good," Orange said. "She did her research on succinylcholine, did her research on the how quickly a body burns. But she did not know how to stage a killing."

Kim had left empty beer bottles in the room and a pack of cigars. The cigars would be the clue that blew Kim's story up in smoke.

Steve was not a smoker and the cigars she had left behind as evidence were not the kind to start a fire.

"There was an investigation as to how a fire like this could have started," prosecuting attorney Robert Dean said. "That fire could not have started by the ashes of a cigar."

Kim would state that after she and Steve had gotten into a fight she went for a drive. She wanted to visit Mike and Maureen Miller who only lived minutes away. She stated she had become lost. The prosecution thought that her excuse seemed odd as she had visited the Millers on numerous occasions. She also had a brother who lived only a few blocks away from the Miller home. And why had she not simply called them on her cell phone?

"I didn't want to wake anyone," Kim said when asked why she didn't call.

Her answer was incongruent as why would she worry about waking someone up with a cell phone call when she didn't have a problem arriving on their doorstep in the middle of the night?

Nine days after the murder, police would arrive at the home of a Hricko friend where Kim had been staying. They had a search warrant for her car but Kim felt the noose tightening around her neck. She ran to the bathroom room and locked it behind herself as the police entered the home.

Kim then swallowed a whole bottle of Xanax.

"Come out of there, Kim," the police yelled.

They busted the door down and saw Kim there in the bathtub, holding a razor blade over her wrist.

"I'll kill myself!" she screamed. "I'll fucking do it!"

The officers quickly subdued Kim without further incident. They then transported her to a psychiatric facility where she was put on suicide watch.

The trial would only last six days as the prosecuting attorney detailed how Kim staged the murder.

"She stated that he was sloppy drunk," prosecuting attorney Robert Dean said. "And that he wanted to have sex. She said they got into an argument and that she left for a few hours. She said she drove around and got lost. And then she returned to the cottage and saw that it was full of smoke and then she reported that the room was on fire."

The case against Kim was made by several friends, co-workers, and neighbors. They all testified about the affair, the plot to kill Steve and her desire to acquire the drug succinylcholine.

Kim Hricko would be found guilty of murder and arson. She would be sentenced to life in prison.

"It's sad that he (Steve) is not the one in the world anymore and she is," Maureen said.

"He was my best friend," Mike said. "And the fact that he isn't here anymore is pretty hard for me to take."

The other victim aside from Steve was their nine-year-old daughter. She lost both her father and her mother.

"Her child is the victim," Maureen said. "And is forever going to wonder which side of the family is telling the truth. Is it true that her mother was unjustly accused or is it true that she's a cold, manipulating, calculating murderer."

END

LOUISA MERRIFIELD : POISON KILLER

ANA BENSON

Louisa Merrifield Biography

There is an ongoing myth that if a woman wants to murder someone, she will use poison. These claims are partially true because 40% of killers who used poison are female. Surely, women do have more opportunities to administer the dangerous concoction to their victims because they are the caregivers. The women cook food, take care of a household, etc. And in the past, poison was simply laying around in forms of different cleaning agents and rodenticides.

The poisoners would often benefit from their victim's death, and this happened in the case of Louisa Merrifield, also known as the Blackpool Poisoner. She wanted to inherit a nice property in a wealthy part of the town, and Sarah Ricketts was in her way.

Early life

Louisa May was born in 1909 in Wigan, United Kingdom. Her father was a Methodist minister while her mother stayed at home in order to take care of the family. Louisa May grew up in a very religious environment, and her father was quite strict. She didn't have the freedom to do what she wanted which resulted in Louisa's unhappy adolescence. The same feeling stayed with her throughout her life. Louisa May didn't finish school so she didn't get the proper education which could have improved her status. After all, her father didn't allow it because it was uncommon for girls to attend colleges back in the day. Louisa May was supposed to be just like her mother and manage the household.

Louisa was very unlucky in terms of the relationships as well. She wasn't an attractive woman. As a matter of fact, Louisa was short and stocky, so there weren't a lot of suitors coming her way. But she did marry a man called Joseph who was an ironworker. Joseph was a heavy drinker who would spend the majority of his days either at work or in a local pub. The couple had four children together. The marriage lasted until Joseph's death from liver failure. His body simply couldn't take the amount of alcohol he drank regularly. Louisa hated being married to

Joseph, and she eventually admitted to her friends that she felt relieved when he died.

It took Louisa only three months to find a new husband. The recent widow chose her lodger who was seventy-eight years old. Louisa was in her thirties, but she clearly wasn't bothered by this age difference. The lodger's name was Richard Watson, and the two were married for only two months. Richard suffered a fatal heart attack, making Louisa a widow for the second time. Having in mind the events that would occur later, some investigators did take a closer look at Richard's death but found nothing suspicious about it. The man was almost eighty years old, and it is very likely that he died from natural causes.

Louisa May wasn't a wealthy woman, but she longed for the money and the easy life. She often struggled to put the food on the table and wanted to provide the necessities to all of her four children. Since she couldn't find a way to earn more money from her work, Louisa decided to commit a ration book fraud. The entire country was in the war, and the supplies were sparse. Ration books were used in order to even the field and provide every family with just enough food, clothes, and other useful goods. But Louisa wasn't happy with the amount her family was getting. So she managed to put her hands on a total of seven ration books, giving her more than enough supplies. However, her crime was soon discovered which lead to a quick arrest.

The war was coming to an end, and the United Kingdom started dealing with the criminals who abused the post-conflict situation in the country. Louisa May was sentenced to 84 days in prison and she was locked up in 1946. That wasn't the end of her ordeal because as soon as she was released, three of her children were taken away from her. The government decided that she was an unfit mother and that the children should be placed in the institutions because they will give them all the care they needed. Left on her own, Louisa May felt lost. With two failed marriages behind her, she started thinking about tying the knot once again.

Marriage to Alfred Merrifield

Louisa May was forty-six years old when she decided to marry Alfred Merrifield. He lived in Blackpool and was a pensioner. Alfred was significantly older than Louisa and he was in his sixties. The man was in good health, except for the fact that he was slightly deaf. It is suspected that Louisa selected Alfred because she thought that there is no way someone her age would be interested in her. As previously mentioned, she considered herself to be below average when it comes to physical appearance, and the years haven't been kind to her either. She was a bit overweight and starting to lose her sight. Louisa had to wear thick eyeglasses in order to function properly.

Alfred was a mild-mannered man who liked Louisa a lot. She would later tell her friends that Alfred pursued her for months until she finally agreed to become his wife. It was clear that Alfred's money wasn't the motivation because his overall income was very low. The newlyweds struggled a lot from the very beginning of their marriage. The financial problems weren't something uncommon for Louisa, so she did her best to find more work. Alfred tried to help her out a bit, but no one would offer him any temporary work position.

The only thing Louisa did well was housekeeping. After all, she did take care of her family for years. She applied for various cooking jobs, as well as for nursing positions, but she would often get fired. Her past employers described her as a difficult woman who would often argue with her supervisors. Louisa also drank a lot, which was a habit she picked up from her first husband. Alfred and Louisa simply couldn't make things work when it came to the finances. His pension was too low, and she kept losing the jobs. In the end, they started selling or pawning their possessions in hopes they would be able to survive a month. It was a difficult life filled with ups and downs. They needed a break as soon as possible because worrying if they will have enough money to buy food next week was tiring. Therefore, Louisa Merrifield grabbed the local newspapers in hopes of finding any type of work that would fit her experience and qualifications. She saw an interesting ad in Lancashire Evening Gazette, and things quickly moved forward.

Meeting Sarah Ricketts

Blackpool is a well-known vacation spot in the United Kingdom. Overall, the city is quite wealthy due to the tourists who frequent this place in the warmer months. Sarah Ricketts was a middle-class woman and a widow. She lived alone in a bungalow in Blackpool, which was located at 339 Devonshire Road. The house was in a part of the city called Norbreck which housed many prominent families that lived in the area. The woman had plenty of money and could afford to have a live-in housekeeper who would take care of both her and the household. Sarah was disabled, and she needed help as well as the company. Considering the location and the terms, Sarah Ricketts expected that many people would respond to her newspaper ad. She was looking for a housekeeper and a handyman who would live on her property.

But Sarah was infamous for her behavior, and the majority of candidates were not willing to deal with her. As previously stated, she had plenty of money in her bank account, but Sarah still acted like a middle-class woman. The widow was quite short and tiny, but she would intimidate anyone around her with her fiery temper. She was a difficult woman, and her dietary habits were particularly strange. As a matter of fact, she loved to eat jam, often straight out of the jar. Afterwards, she would have rum and stout. Having in mind that Sarah Ricketts was seventy-nine years old, her food preferences were very odd.

Sarah Ricketts needed reliable help around the house, and as she was reviewing the applications, Louisa Merrifield's immediately stood out. She was married to Alfred Merrifield so Sarah thought that he would be a great addition to the household as well. After all, he would be able to fix things around the bungalow. Sarah didn't know that Louisa Merrifield had a sketchy history. It was omitted from the application because Louisa's goal was to present herself in the best possible light. Sarah's rushed decision eventually had terrible consequences.

Louisa and Alfred Merrifield accepted Sarah's invitation to work for her, and the couple arrived at the bungalow on 12th March 1953. Things were looking great in the first couple of weeks, and Sarah was happy with her choice. Louisa was fairly young and able to take care of Sarah. Her cooking was great, and Sarah enjoyed the meals Louisa would prepare on a daily basis. Alfred was in charge of the gardening, and he cleared out the overgrown area, making the front yard beautiful once again. Sarah was ecstatic, and she started trusting her live-in housemates.

The entire neighborhood knew how happy Sarah was with her choice because she didn't hesitate to talk about them to her friends. She even gave Louisa her checkbook in order to pay the bills without thinking twice about the possibility that the woman might abuse this power, and steal her money. But the tensions started to rise very soon. Sarah began complaining that Louisa is not feeding her well. Apparently, Louisa's meals were starting to get sparse and Sarah was used to eating more food. She attacked Louisa that she was spending the food money on alcohol instead of buying quality ingredients for the kitchen.

The arguments were frequent, but this didn't stop Louisa and Alfred to approach Sarah's family doctor. Louisa was certain that Sarah liked her and appreciated the help she had provided so far. Apparently, the elderly lady wanted to write a new will, and she needed to get the doctor's permission that she is sane and clear-minded. The doctor was taken aback by this request, but having in mind that Sarah Ricketts lived alone and had two estranged daughters, he thought that she really liked her new housekeepers, and felt the need to leave them her bungalow, as well as the rest of the property. The bungalow was worth £3000, which is somewhere around $119,000 in today's currency.

The woman seemed coherent, and her solicitor was summoned to her bungalow as well. Sarah told him that Alfred and Louisa were good people who deeply cared about her wellbeing and that she wishes to leave them her property. She thought they do an excellent job around the house regardless of their tiny quarrels and that they deserve to inherit the property after her death. The solicitor wrote down the changes. Since he didn't sense any danger behind this request and the woman seemed completely sane, the doctor gave his approval, and a new will was made on 9th April 1953.

Sarah had a tendency to change her testament every now and then because she was often getting into fights with her two adult daughters. The woman thought they were after her money and would do her best to blackmail the two by denying them the property. As soon as Sarah Ricketts made a new will, Louisa started plotting how to kill the elderly woman. She traveled all the way to Manchester with her husband in order to get the things she needed and put her plan into motion. Alfred was very friendly to the clerk who worked at the store, and the man remembered him afterward. The two of them talked about health problems, including Alfred's deafness. The clerk didn't ask them where they were from, but the fact that they traveled for an hour to buy rat poison which is sold almost everywhere might have raised a flag right there on the spot.

The poison was a powerful concoction called Rodine, and it was used for eliminating rats from the households. The poison itself is quite strong due to the amount of white phosphorous it used to contain back in the days. Rodine is still sold today, but the formula had drastically changed. White phosphorous can be found in different military weapons, such as incendiary munition because it burns brightly and quickly. It can be quite damaging to humans, especially if one ingests it. As a matter of fact, 15mg of white phosphorous is enough to kill an adult. It is very toxic and can damage liver, heart, and kidneys. White phosphorous can be easily detected because the body might give a bit of a glow if someone managed to get this chemical into their system. The majority of people will notice a strong smell of garlic around white phosphorous as well. Rodine was a popular way of getting rid of rats, mostly due to its efficiency, so having it around the house wasn't an unusual thing.

The poisoning

Things really started to change during April because Louisa was quite unhappy with her job. She started complaining to everyone who would listen to her about how difficult Sarah Ricketts was. As a matter of fact, Louisa painted her as a very complicated person who would complain about the smallest things. Since the woman was partially paralyzed, she didn't move around too often. However, Louisa told her acquaintances that Sarah would simply ignore the fact that she cannot walk on her own and call them up in the middle of the night because she needed help getting out of the bed. Louisa was also annoyed because Sarah told her that her cooking was horrible, and she eventually started refusing to eat altogether.

Louisa was apparently disappointed in Sarah because she told the delivery man who brought her a supply of alcohol that the couple was spending too much money on themselves and that she would very likely fire them soon. Louisa claimed that wasn't true, and that Sarah was simply being mean to them even though they were doing their best to provide her with the best care possible. The following days were very confusing because Louisa mentioned to a couple of neighbors that Sarah died. It was evident that she was still alive and in the house. When confronted with making false claims, Louisa simply told her friends: *"She's not dead yet, but she soon will be."* Surely enough, her sinister predictions will come true more sooner than later.

It was 13th of April when Louisa Merrifield decided that it was time to remove Sarah Ricketts from the picture. She prepared Sarah favorite meal and added a couple of spoons of Rodine to the jam. The woman started feeling sick right away because the dosage was very strong. As a matter of fact, Sarah was in unbelievable pain minutes after her meal. Unable to figure out what was going on, Sarah thought that she might be having digestion problems. Louisa helped her get to the bathroom, but Sarah was not feeling any better. She cried while in there, and her screams could be heard throughout the bungalow. Four hours have gone by, and Sarah completely lost the power of speech, unable to scream or speak to anyone. Five hours later Sarah Ricketts passed away. She died on 14th April 1953.

Louisa contacted Doctor Wood in order to report that Sarah is not feeling well. She didn't specify what exactly was happening with the woman. Even though Sarah Ricketts was old, she was fairly healthy. The woman didn't suffer from any chronic diseases, and the only thing that was sometimes problematic was bronchitis. However, it wasn't that frequent, so Doctor Wood didn't visit Sarah's home often. Since there was no hurry, the doctor decided to postpone his visit to the Ricketts' residence. But surprisingly, Sarah died the following morning. Knowing her history, Doctor Wood was certain right away that something was wrong. Yes, the woman was in her eighties, but she was perfectly fine the last time he examined her.

His suspicions were supported by Doctor Yule, who did a check-up on Sarah only a couple of days prior to her death because the housekeepers were asking for an approval in order to modify the woman's will. He asked the Merrifields what happened, and Louisa admitted that Sarah started feeling ill one day before her death, but she decided to contact Doctor Wood instead. According to her, she thought that he might feel agitated due to the fact that he already examined Sarah Ricketts recently. Louisa didn't fail to mention that Sarah wished to be cremated as soon as possible after her death. Doctor Yule found this even more strange because he knew the woman, and she never expressed her willingness to be sent away like that.

The autopsy

The entire situation was getting stranger as the more information came his way. Doctor Yule decided not to cremate Sarah's body, but to analyze it thoroughly instead. The law back then was not to issue a death certificate if anything seemed suspicious. The symptoms which were described by Louisa were very odd, and he needed to confirm that the woman wasn't killed. Doctor Yule decided to send Sarah's body to a coroner who would do a full autopsy.

After testing the tissues for any trace of poison, the coroner discovered high levels of white phosphorous in her liver. When he opened up the body, the internal organs had a faint glow to them which was quite alarming. Not to forget the garlic odor that filled out the room. This confirmed that Sarah died of phosphorous poisoning. Doctor Yule's concerns were confirmed, and now he knew that Sarah Ricketts was poisoned. He immediately alerted the authorities who zeroed in on her caretakers because they were always in contact with the woman, and had numerous opportunities to poison Sarah. After all, they were cooking her the meals and preparing food on a daily basis.

The investigation

Louisa and Alfred Merrifield worked for Sarah Ricketts for just over a month, and the woman clearly didn't know them well. They were the prime suspects from the very beginning, so the police started monitoring their steps very carefully. There were so many details that indicated that something was very wrong with Sarah's death. For instance, Louisa didn't feel sad when the woman passed away. Unsurprisingly to the law enforcement, she was excited because the bungalow belonged to her. Louisa was happy so she would constantly brag to her friends. Having in mind the peculiar way Sarah Ricketts died, the reporters approached Louisa a couple of weeks later to ask for a statement. She mostly focused on how much she disliked her husband, and that he was very boring. Louisa even implicated that he might have had an affair with Sarah which was completely untrue.

The police were familiar with the poison which was used in this murder, so they decided to search the bungalow in order to confirm it was available to Louisa Merrifield. After combing through the financial statements, they have discovered that the couple traveled to Manchester a few days before the murder. The police located the shop in which Rodine was bought, and they talked to the clerk who remembered talking to Alfred on that day. But this was still pretty normal due to the fact that numerous people used Rodine every single day. But knowing that the couple bought a full can of this poison gave them an advantage. The investigators thought that there should be more Rodine left in the bungalow because there is no need to use a whole can in just a couple of weeks. The poison is very efficient, and the can should still be in the bungalow unless they were covering up their tracks and getting rid of the evidence.

After a thorough search of the premises, the police officers didn't find a can of Rodine which suggested that the couple has thrown it away in hopes of not being discovered. Louisa and Alfred were in serious trouble because they remained the only suspects, and the police decided to arrest them right away. All the evidence were against them, and the fact that the United Kingdom still had a death penalty indicated that they might be facing this punishment.

The arrests and trial

Both Louisa and Alfred were brought to the station soon after the search of the bungalow was complete. When presented with the evidence, the investigators saw a change in Louisa's behavior. They told her about numerous interviews that proved she had talked about the death of Sarah Ricketts even before the poison was administered. Louisa tried blaming her husband, but this plan didn't work out well either. During Alfred's interview, the investigators did think that the old man was forced to follow Louisa's lead. He was deaf, and couldn't remember some of the key details of the whole incident. While the majority of detectives might think that the man was trying to save himself from the death sentence, the investigators working on this case actually believed that Alfred had little knowledge of the crime before it occurred.

Louisa and Alfred were brought to trial in July of 1953. Louisa defended herself by saying that Alfred cheated on her with Sarah Ricketts and that the two of them had a sexual relationship. Alfred once again had no knowledge of this, and the judge was certain that the man wasn't involved in the murder plot. Louisa continued to incriminate herself even further by refusing to admit that she talked about Sarah's death days before it really happened. However, multiple witnesses have confirmed this, and it was improbable that more than one person misheard her. Not to forget Louisa's behavior after Sarah's death.

The trial lasted for a total of nine days, and Louisa stuck to her defense that Alfred was having an affair with Sarah. However, the judge dismissed these claims, saying that Louisa is 'a vulgar and stupid woman with a dirty mind.' Louisa was found guilty of a first-degree murder and was sentenced to a death penalty by hanging. The judge was unsure what to do with Alfred because it was obvious that the old man didn't participate in the planning or the execution of the murder. In the end, the judge decided to drop the charges against Alfred Merrifield.

The aftermath

The public all around the United Kingdom wanted to know more about the Blackpool Poisoner, which was the nickname given to Louisa by the press. Everyone eagerly waited to hear what Alfred had to say about the murder and his wife Louisa. Since he was named as a beneficiary in Sarah's will, Alfred moved into the bungalow because it now legally belonged to him. He agreed to give an interview to national newspapers in which he talked about his marriage to Louisa. He admitted that he was very afraid for his own life because she had taken out a total of seven insurance policies on him. He was certain that she would have poisoned him as well if she wasn't in prison. Not to forget that Alfred admitted that Louisa abused him during their marriage which resulted in his bad health.

Louisa Merrifield was held in Strangeways Prison in Manchester. The judge has sent an official letter to the most famous hangman in the United Kingdom, and his name was Albert Pierrepoint. Pierrepoint accepted to be Louisa's executioner. He was experienced and didn't hesitate to execute women. The death penalty took place on 18th of September 1953 which was six months after the murder. She was the last woman hanged at Strangeways Prison. Louisa was buried inside the prison walls. Alfred did visit her twice before her death.

Alfred Merrifield continued living in Sarah Ricketts' bungalow for years after the poisoning, but the court ordered him to move out eventually. He continued to struggle financially and even appeared in local sideshows a couple of times. Alfred was eighty years old when he died in 1962.

KILLER CHURCH LADY : THE TRUE STORY OF BLANCHE MOORE

KATIE STONE

"People couldn't believe that she did what she did. People became fascinated that how could someone who on the surface could be so nice, could be capable of such a heinous crime." - Paula Orange

Blanche Taylor Moore was born on February 17th, 1933 in North Carolina, the fifth of seven children. Her father was Parker Davis Kiser, a self-taught minister who had both a drinking and gambling problem. Her mother, Flonnie Honeycutt, held little sway in the goings on in the Kiser household. Flonnie would work in the local mills, bringing home $40 a week. She turned the money over to her husband who promptly turned around and spent the money on younger women. Kiser did various odd jobs to support the family, primarily working in a saw mill then later as an insurance salesman. His primary occupation, however, was the seduction of women that he came across in both bars and churches.

The Reverend Kiser was a strict father and didn't allow any of his children to participate in school activities or spend hanging out with friends.

Living a double life, P.D. Kiser's gambling debts increased to the point where he made the decision to sell young Blanche off as a prostitute to pay off his debts which he incurred during card games.

After one losing streak, Reverend Kiser took his adolescent daughter for a drive and pulled over to the side of the road.

"I'm going to pull up under that tree," Kiser said. "When I do, I want you to go fuck that man."

"P.D. Kiser was an alcoholic and self-righteous country minister," said psychologist Kelleher. "Despite efforts to abstain from alcohol he always relapsed. Blanche's childhood was utterly destroyed by her father and she lived in a childhood prison of despair."

Blanche, desperate to leave the abusive household, married James Taylor in May of 1952. Blanche was nineteen years old at the time,

Taylor was twenty-four. She would give birth to their first daughter, Vanessa, in 1953.

Blanche was the typical Southern diva, confident in her ability to seduce any man she wanted but found the pickings slim in her small North Carolina town. She was attractive by most accounts, having long black hair and eyes that "were so dark they looked black."

"Blanche's face was sculpted in the high bird-boned features of the very prettiest Appalachian women," one researcher said. "Long, lithe, with generous breasts and a sleek round bottom perched on slender, perfectly shaped legs."

"She flew her small burgh of Tarheel by grabbing the first man who asked her to marry him. Young Blanche was left with one overwhelming wish for the future-to leave her perverse, sermonizing father and begin a new life that was far away from his abuse."

Finances were tough and Blanche was forced to work as a cashier at the Kroger supermarket. She would toil on the job for six years before giving birth to their second child, Cindi, in 1953. Still, she became a popular fixture at the market as folks would line up at her register just to have a quick chat with the friendly Blanche. She would remain a mainstay at the supermarket for decades.

"She was always friendly to customers and her co-workers," a former Kroger employee said. "You would have never guessed her as being unhappy or mean to anyone. Just wasn't in her."

Her tenure at Kroger's looked to be mixed, however, as Blanche could be moody. But the management hierarchy gave her high marks in her job performance and labeled her as a "good leader" as she trained other grocery checkers.

Still, a dark side emerged.

"She could be vindictive," said one co-worker who asked not to be identified. "If you got on her bad side, watch out. She was two-faced. Two-faced and underhanded. There was one incident where a large bag of cash wound up missing. Management would have to explain why her store was the only store that didn't turn a profit."

BAD MARRIAGE

By 1959, things had soured at the homefront. Blanche and James had several loud fights in public. Blanche was dragged behind a car on one occasion and in another she was confronted about an affair with a customer at the Kroger supermarket.

Despite her peculiar manner, Blanche would be promoted to "head cashier" which was the equivalent of a store manager in today's corporate climate. This was one of the few top positions open to Kroger's women employees at that time. She would also sell Tupperware at home parties which she used as a cover to seduce different men that interested her.

Her husband James seemed powerless against the woman he married. He worked as a furniture restorer but jobs were few and far between for the former military veteran who had just returned from the Korean War. James was described as a "burly man" that was "quick to anger." He spent the majority of his time editing sermons taken from the Glen Hope Baptist church and sending them overseas for missionaries to spread the gospel. He also began drowning himself in alcohol which was much to Blanche's disappointment.

"Blanche had, in essence, married a carbon copy of her father," forensic psychologist Paula Orange said. "James was like her dad in that he was a compulsive gambler and was horrible with money. He would disappear on the weekend and come back flat broke."

Her own father wouldn't behave much better, leaving Blanche's mother in 1960 as he vowed to "find himself a younger woman."

Blanche then acted out on her own. She continued to use the supermarket as her own personal singles bar, having affairs with numerous customers and male supervisors.

James would find out about her affairs and would threaten to leave Blanche. The two would continue to have violent, explosive arguments but ultimately James would never follow through on his threats to leave.

A NEW MAN

By 1962, however, Blanche would have her sights set on a new assistant manager by the name of Raymond Reid.

Reid was already married with two young children and initially spurned the advances of the slightly older Blanche.

But what Blanche wanted, Blanche got. It took three years of flirting to finally get Raymond to lower his guard. Blanche seduced the married man but continued to sleep with other male companions she met through the store.

To further complicate her life, Blanche's father had taken ill shortly after she arrived to make some sort of attempt at reconciliation.

Blanche remained at his bedside and helped to try and nurse him back to health. The elder Kiser, however, was too far gone. He died due to "heart attack triggered by chronic emphysema."

Doctors completely overlooked the fact that Kiser had suffered from violent stomach cramps, diarrhea, vomiting, delirium and a blue skin pallor.

This all pointed to death by arsenic poisoning but they had no reason to suspect Blanche of anything.

Noting the ease with she got away with her father's death, Blanche set her sights on the other man who was an obstacle to her happiness.

Her husband, James Taylor would suffer a near-fatal heart attack. His brush with death forced him to "get right with God" and he attempted to reconcile with Blanche.

"James Taylor's life trajectory was strikingly similar to that of Blanche's father, Parker Davis," Orange said. "Like Davis, he would find religion later in life and put on the pretense of a changed man. Blanche saw through it all, she herself was used to men using religion as a prop much like her father. But she put up appearances for appearance sake."

Blanche would later describe James as becoming "the perfect husband and father" but her six-year affair with Raymond Reid continued.

Despite their marital infidelity, Blanche would try and persuade Reid to attend church with her.

"I have been quite religious all my life, or I was," Blanche recalled. "I was very active in the First Disciples until the fire. After that, I just lost my interest in religion."

With his wife deeply entrenched in an affair, James would come down with the "flu" in September of 1970. He started to lose his hair, had diarrhea, swollen glands, blood stool and blue skin pallor. All the signs of arsenic poisoning yet no one who examined him was any the wiser. He would be hospitalized at the end of the month and die a few dies after his admission, shortly after Blanche brought him some ice cream.

Blanche would then help take care of James' mother, Isla, up until her death on November 25th, 1970. Doctors signed off on Isla's death as something attributed to natural causes. Inexplicably, they ignored the blue skin pallor on the woman as well as the undigested arsenic that remained in the Blanche's mother-in-law's stomach.

So within two months, Blanche had eliminated both her husband James and her mother-in-law, Isla. She was able to obtain a small portion of their estate and used the money to buy a home in Burlington, North Carolina.

Despite proceeds from these deaths, her co-workers thought she may have been "tapping the till" at work as there was no way she could afford such a home on the meager inheritance.

COAST IS CLEAR

Raymond Reid would decide to go all in on his affair with Blanche. He left his wife and children in 1971, a full nine years after first meeting Blanche. He got himself a small apartment and filed for divorce from his wife, fully expecting Blanche to become his bride.

Blanche would stop by at Reid's new place, cook him breakfast and sexually entertain him. She said that Reid was "helpless" without her.

This caused a stir not only in their workplace but in the small town in which they both lived.

"Mom never expected to spend the rest of her life by herself. She had too much to offer," said Blanche's daughter Cynthia Chatman.

"Reid was a very good man. He was good to us," said Vanessa, Blanche's other daughter.

Blanche herself didn't feel that way. As a future district attorney said while investigating Blanche's story, she would soon deem the young Reid as someone who "wasn't good enough, she wanted to date someone better. She was very blunt about that."

Blanche had a foul mouth and often said things that were inappropriate. Once she told the friend of her son-in-law, "you know what you really need? You need a really good blow job. If I went down on you, it'd probably kill you. You probably couldn't handle it."

She wouldn't limit her romantic encounters with the male supervisors like Reid at the supermarket. She targeted anyone she found handsome as when a new delivery man entered the store, Blanche said, "Man, I'd like to see the dick on that guy."

SEXUAL HARASSMENT

The highly sexual Blanche would claim sexual harassment during her tenure at Kroger's. A top company official named Robert J. Hutton paid a visit to her store. Blanche would contend that he made advances and fondled female cashiers.

"He reached him up my dress, exposed himself and grabbed my buttocks," Blanche said as she recalled an encounter with Hutton. "He had his pants down and asked 'Are you ready for this?'"

Blanche then picked up Hutton's pants and underwear as she fled from the store. EmbaRrassed, Hutton had to borrow a meat cutter's smock before exiting the store.

Blanche didn't return to Kroger's after the incident. She filed a sexual harassment suit and began seeing psychiatrists. One of her doctors, Dr. Jesse N. McNeil said in an affidavit that Blanche suffered from "depression, anxiety, and a serious suicidal condition. She felt completely alienated and antagonistic toward men and has not been able to maintain any meaningful social contacts with members of the opposite sex.

Her defense attorney would later dismiss the affidavit as "hyperbole" to bolster the charges of the sexual harassment suit.

It would later be revealed that Blanche had a flirtatious relationship with Hutton before she filed suit. She was on the lookout for someone "better" than Reid and thought that Hutton may fit the bill. But the relationship soured and Hutton ultimately lost his job.

Kroger would settle out of court with Blanche, paying the flirtatious young cashier a lump-sum payment of $275,000.

YET ANOTHER RUSE

Always on the look out for "quick cash," Blanche concocted a scheme to collect some fire insurance in 1985. A mysterious fire broke out at her home and Blanche put the blame on a local "pervert", a man that she claimed to have seen lurking around her property.

"I saw a man," Blanche said. "He was creeping around the side wall."

"Did you call the cops?"

"No," Blanche said. "He was, you know, touching himself. Touching himself down there. I screamed and he ran away."

Firefighters agreed that arson was the cause and did not question her tale of the unknown "pervert" who set her home ablaze. Blanche would take the proceeds from the fire insurance and purchase a mobile home.

A month later, however, the mobile home was burned to the ground. Blanche once again blamed a "pervert" whom she said followed her to the trailer home. The authorities believed her and she collected another fire insurance check.

"Really not sure what Blanche was doing with all this money," Orange said. "She had to have over a quarter of a million dollars on hand from inheritances and sexual harassment suits. She soon realized that money could be gained quicker through settlements as opposed to hard work."

Still on the lookout for a "new man," Blanche met the acquaintance of the Reverend Dwight Moore on Easter Sunday of 1985.

Moore was the pastor of the Carolina United Church of Christ. Divorced with two grown children of his own, the fifty-one-year-old preacher immediately caught the eye of the forty-two-year-old Blanche.

She introduced herself at the end of his sermon and complimented him on his speaking ability. He soon began "counseling" her as her impending lawsuit with Kroger came to a head.

The two got to know each other and Blanche was judgmental toward the Reverend when she found out that his own marriage ended when he was discovered to have an affair with another woman in his church. But Moore was taken by the beauty and Southern charm of Blanche and would not be denied.

"Moore saw Blanche as the innocent victim," Orange said. "She could do no wrong in his eyes and this blinded him to a lot of things, mainly the fact that she had instigated the flirtation and was still involved with Reid. And oh yeah, she just killed her husband. But Blanche saw opportunity in the Reverend. The preacher man was divorced and the pastor of a relatively small church. So she probably saw authority in that. She liked men in the authority, whether it be a manager at Kroger's or a man giving a sermon in a small church."

It began platonic enough, at first, the two began meeting for lunch then dinner on a "friends" basis. Blanche did begin dropping hints that they shouldn't be surprised if she married a "preacher man" in the near future.

"The Reverend was putty in the hands of a seductress like Blanche," Orange said. "Blanche could quote scripture then talk explicitly about sex. She put up a false front of a churchgoing woman but had a carnal way about her. The Reverend took one look at her and thought to himself 'we got a live one here!'"

Moore was smitten and his phone calls to Blanche increased over time. He would leave notes on Blanche's front door step which were sometimes intercepted by Blanche's daughters.

The Reverend would invite Blanche out to "get some ice cream" and the two would soon arrive together as church gatherings.

"She was dating both both the Reverend Moore and Raymond Reid," Orange said. "Her daughters believed that her relationship with Reid had cooled off but nobody told Raymond. Moore seemed none the wiser that Blanche was still seeing Reid. So Blanche was playing both sides against the other. If things worked out with the Reverend she would dump Reid."

Reid would not go away easy. He had abandoned his own wife over twelve years earlier in the hopes of eventually marrying Blanche.

"She couldn't just break-up with Reid," Orange said. "She was in too deep. She got to know his family and friends. The expectation was that they were going to get married but for whatever reason in Blanche's mind, she held out. So, rather than string him along further she decided to eliminate him from the equation."

Reid came down with a case of the "shingles" in 1986 as he developed a skin condition that would point to arsenical peripheral neuritis.

By April, he would be hospitalized with the same symptoms as Blanche's previous victims. This would include diarrhea, projectile vomiting and a loss of sensation in both his hands and feet.

Again, physicians dropped the ball in assessing these classic warning signs of arsenic poisoning. The doctors ordered special tests for "heavy metals intoxication" as well as a urine test which showed six times the normal amount of arsenic in Reid's system.

The report never reached the desk of the doctor's and Reid would continue to suffer.

Blanche would play the role of the dutiful girlfriend but again her inappropriate comments would be put on display when on occasion Reid's son Steve left the room with an attractive young woman. When the young man returned, Blanche asked: "Well, did you fuck her?"

The young man looked on in shock then denied the accusation.

"Well, why not? Growing boy your age needs some pussy once in a while. What's the last time you had some good pussy?"

DEVOTED GIRLFRIEND

When she wasn't harassing Reid's young son, Blanche would be by the side of the sick man on a daily basis. She put on a false front to Reid and his nurses, quoting the Bible and giving the impression that she was a compassionate, Christian woman attending to the needs of her boyfriend.

"She made quite an impression on the nurses on duty," Orange said. "They would testify later that she was the epitome of the caring girlfriend. She showed the man compassion and caring and the all thought that he was very lucky to have Blanche Taylor Moore in his life."

Reid would be diagnosed with Guillain-Barre Syndrome, an auto-immune disorder with the symptoms being muscle weakness, nerve-tingling and progressive fatigue.

"Raymond would die and be revived again," Orange said. "His heart failed and he would be declared clinically dead, losing heartbeat and respiration but the medical staff was able to revive him."

Blanche, however, would be waiting to provide "care" after the staff saved her boyfriend's life. She would come with a cup of processed food and eagerly feed Reed after his latest return from the dead. She would make a show of giving Reid her homemade pudding and specially made "milkshakes".

"Her demeanor was so sweet and unassuming that the nurses wouldn't even think of questioning her," Orange said. "They would nurse Reid back to health, get some of that poison out of his system then Blanche would come into the room with her 'concoctions.' It was literally one step forward and ten steps back for the poor man."

Raymond would recuperate then relapse again into respiratory arrest.

"Think of the worst flu you've ever had then multiply it by ten," Orange said. "Then you're resuscitated again and again. He was on a roller coaster for his life. Absolutely horrific. All the while, Blanche would witness Reid's battles with death. She knew she was the cause of it, with her arsenic milkshakes and pudding, yet she would stand there aghast, praying to the God above that Reid be delivered from the illness."

Reid would regain consciousness but remain confused. He would then began to recuperate and get his senses back. He would feel optimistic about his chances then he would relapse again.

Physical and psychological torture on repeat play.

This would continue for three months. Blanche seized the opportunity to have Reid create a living will. She named herself as executor and beneficiary to one-third of Reid's estate. The other two-thirds would be divided between his sons.

"Blanche had a way about her," Orange said. "She could talk just about any man into doing anything for her. A great deal of her ability to have gotten away with the things she did was her own persona. By this time, she had killed her father, first husband, and her mother-in-law with the exact same methods. Yet no one ever suspected anything or put two and two together, not even those closest to her. Her persona was so ingratiating and unassuming that it would be unthinkable."

After the will was drawn out, Reid's health rapidly deteriorated. In October of 1986, he was brought into intensive care suffering from renal and respiratory failure. He would die three days later as his body began bloating so severely that his skin ripped apart.

According to her daughters, Blanche seemed torn up that Reid had passed away.

Doctor's blamed Guillain-Barre syndrome but wanted an autopsy to be certain. Blanche declined, manipulating Reid's sons into agreeing with her that no autopsy be performed.

"Blanche was like most serial killers," Orange said. "Narcissistic. She thought she was special. She thought she was smarter than everyone else and that she would never be caught."

This now opened the door to a relationship with the Reverend Moore.

"The coast was clear," Orange said.

The Reverend accompanied Blanche to Reid's funeral. She had acquired over $30,000 from Redis's estate in addition to pilfering his safe deposit box and the safe in his home. Reid's sons also gave Blanche over $45,000 from their father's life insurance in the belief that "he would have wanted it that way."

"Then the Reverend didn't waste any time," Orange said. "After an obligatory period of grieving, the Reverend pursued her with great fervor until she finally relented and the two had a wedding date set for August of 1987, less than ten months after Reid's death. Blanche now had a sizable nest egg but most likely lost it all through audacious spending and mismanagement. She had money acquired from the sexual harassment suit, her first husband, and now money gained through her manipulation of Reid's will. She got addicted to the scheming. The game playing and manipulation. It was all an adrenaline rush to her."

THE PERFECT WOMAN

To Moore's family and friends, Blanche seemed like the perfect woman for him. She put on a front of knowing the Bible backward and forwards, having the personality of a "church lady" to match.

"Behind the scenes," Orange said. "Both the Reverend and Blanche knew better. She was a hot number to be sure and everything that was repressed in the Reverend now came to fore. He would now have his cake and eat it too, the Southern man's dream of having a woman who is a lady in church but a tiger in bed."

Things were looking rosy until Blanche was diagnosed with breast cancer. She had one breast surgically removed in order to stop the spread. She went into recovery and the couple pushed the marriage ceremony back another year, to November 27th, 1988.

Things were still not meant to be, however, as three weeks before the wedding the Reverend Moore came down with a mysterious illness all his own. He suffered from vomiting and diarrhea so severe that he had to be hospitalized. Doctors would discover an "intestinal blockage" in the preacher and he was forced to undergo surgery.

Blanche and the Reverend were finally able to tie the knot in April of 1989.

The wedding was simple and witnessed by only two church members.

"She had on a real pretty dress," Doris Pender said, one of the witnesses. "They were beaming. It seemed like there was electricity there. It seemed like they were very much in love."The two lovebirds would go to Montclair, New Jersey for their honeymoon and also visit the Reverend Moore's first grandchild who had just been born.

The honeymoon would be short-lived as the Reverend Moore collapsed on a homeward bound trip five days later.

"There are two competing stories," Orange said. "One is that he ate a pastry then collapsed. The other is that he was spraying insect repellent on some flowers outside his home. Blanche came back with a chicken sandwich for him which promptly made the Reverend sick."

The symptoms eventually grew worse and the Reverend insisted on going to the hospital. He was admitted to the Alamance County Hospital on April 28th and his conditioned worsened after Blanche delivered some "homemade soup."

The doctors inexplicably sent him home but Moore's condition would worsen after he consumed another one of Blanche's meals. She would then drive him to North Carolina Memorial hospital which refused admittance without a written order from Alamance County.

The Reverend had now retained forty pounds of body fluid while Blanche got the necessary paperwork. She would then relay to the Reverend's family that he "was fine, we're just going to do some tests."

Moore's symptoms mirrored that of Guillain-Barre syndrome, the medical staff became suspicious because of the speed of which the symptoms appeared.

"This go around the medical staff tested him for arsenic poisoning," Orange said. "They found huge doses of the poison in his system and immediately suspected that Blanche had given it to him."

The Reverend fought back successfully against the poison. He was able to recuperate and was released from the hospital.

"Reverend Moore set a medical record," Orange said. "The physicians on duty noted that he had survived a dosage of arsenic higher than anyone on record. There was enough poison to kill a moose. Yet the Reverend survived. Amazing."

The police were summoned and became suspicious when they began investigating the number of people associated with Blanche that had died under similar circumstances.

"She didn't do anything," the Reverend Moore said when asked by the police if he believed that Blanche was to blame for his illness. "No way. Not my Blanche. I think I must have inhaled poison while I was spraying the garden for pests."

But the police saw a pussy-whipped man when they saw one. They proceeded to question Blanche who would deny bringing any food to Raymond Reid while he was hospitalized. The claim was contradicted by hospital staffers who were on hand to witness Blanche force Reid to drink one of her "homemade milkshakes."

Investigating further, authorities found out that Blanche had tried to get the Reverend's pension revised so that she would be the principal beneficiary. Blanche became worried that they would test the Reverend for arsenic poison. She had her husband's hair shaved bald but investigating officials were able to obtain samples from the Reverend's pubic region and tested that.

"Both Dwight (Reverend Moore) and Raymond felt depressed," Blanche said when asked why both of her lovers tested high for arsenic. "They were probably taking arsenic themselves."

Police would charge Blanche with assault and had the body of Reid exhumed on his body, consistent with those found on the body of her first husband, James Taylor.

The chief medical examiner would discover that Reid's illness was not only the cause of arsenic but that he continued to receive the poison while he was in the hospital.

The Reverend would refuse to believe that his wife would do such a thing. It took six weeks but the police finally convinced him otherwise after they exhumed the bodies of Raymond Reid and James Taylor.

"You're lucky," the detective informed him. "Damn lucky you're even alive."

The Reverend then confronted Blanche about the accusations he heard from the police. He informed her that their marriage was over. The decision was an emotionally devastating one for the Reverend as Blanche left his hospital bedside covered in crocodile tears.

MOTIVATION?

The townsfolk and those close to Blanche immediately wanted to know why. Why would such a sweet and unassuming woman commit such diabolical crimes. The district attorney, however, couldn't care less. He just knew that the crimes had taken place.

"We don't have to get into why," the DA said. "When you start looking for a rational motive, you generally start overthinking. I just know that this guy died and the state medical examiner said he had a fatal level of arsenic in him."

Blanche was arrested and charged with the murder of Raymond Reid which the DA felt would be easier to prove than the Reverend's poisoning.

During the trial, which opened in Winston-Salem on October 21st, 1990, Blanche continued to deny giving Reid any food. The state produced over fifty-three witnesses who contradicted her statement. Reid's ex-wife and sons also sued Baptist Hospital for malpractice.

During her trial, jurors would discover how Blanche would kill her victims with kindness. She would place the arsenic in the food she would bring for him until ultimately he died.

"Raymond Reid lay in Baptist Hospital flat on his back, bed sores on his back, completely unable to move, tears in his eyes on the days that this woman who was killing him doesn't come," lead prosecutor Janet Branch told the jury, tears streaming down her face.

"He's crying because his murderer isn't coming to see him! Can you imagine anything more pitiful in this whole world? And he loves her with all his heart. ... But she's running around on him, and she's sleeping with Dwight Moore, and she's going to that hospital."

"I never felt the need for vengeance," Moore said. "I have no desire to see her executed. I don't even object to her efforts to get off death row. I have no feelings against her living out her final days in the most humane way possible."

"The authorities began to realize that they had a serial killer on their hands," Orange said. "They wanted to exhume the bodies of everyone that knew Blanche Taylor Moore in their lives. There was a bit of a hysteria going on. Ultimately, I think the authorities decided not to pursue the matter beyond what they could prove in court. The countless one night stands by Blanche would have been impossible to track considering her tenure at Kroger's."

They would exhume five bodies. Traces of arsenic were found in the bodies of both her first husband and her father.

She was cleared of any wrongdoing in her father's death but many believed that the trauma she suffered at the hands of her father led to her becoming a serial killer.

"Her father was a womanizer," Orange said. "And he had abandoned the family had some point. I think that perhaps she mirrored his behavior in her own life and took it a step further, taking out revenge on her father with the many men she came into contact with."

"It certainly isn't uncommon for female serial killers to carry bad relationships with their father into their future relationships with men."

"She is killing her father over and over again."

"I have no doubts as to her guilt," the Reverend Moore said. "The worst lingering effect has been tremors in my hands and weakness in my legs along with peripheral neuropathy. My feet and legs are pretty much a constant reminder (of Blanche).

Blanche Taylor Moore remains on death row in North Carolina. She is the oldest inmate on death row in the state.